Finding My Way Back t

D0484904

A Memoir
By Beverley Lehman West

Finding My Way Back to 1950s Paris

A Memoir

By Beverley Lehman West

For Sally —
Remembering
good times.

Beverley

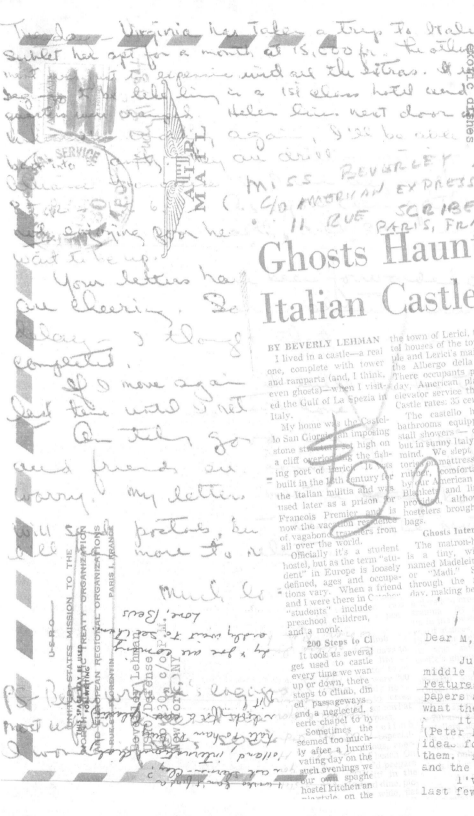

Ghosts Haunt Italian Castle

BY BEVERLY LEHMAN

I lived in a castle—a real one, complete with tower and ramparts (and, I think, even ghosts)—when I visited the Gulf of La Spezia in Italy.

My home was the Castello San Giorgio, an imposing stone structure set high on a cliff overlooking the fishing port of Lerici. It was built in the 13th century for the Italian militia and was used later as a prison for Francois Premier and is now the vacation residence of vagabond travelers from all over the world.

Officially it's a student hostel, but as the term "student" in Europe is loosely defined, ages and occupations vary. When a friend and I were there in October "students" include preschool children, and a monk.

200 Steps to Cl

It took us several get used to castle every time we wan up or down, there steps to climb, din ed passageways and a neglected, eerie chapel to by

Sometimes the seemed too much ly after a luxuri vating day on the such evenings we our own spaghe hostel kitchen an

the town of Lerici, the tel houses of the town ple and Lerici's main the Albergo della P: There occupants pay day, American plan, elevator service throu Castle rates: 35 cents.

The castello has bathrooms equipped stall showers — cold but in sunny Italy we mind. We slept in toria mattresses rubber, comfortable by our American sta Blankets and linen provided, although hostelers brought bags.

Ghosts Intervie

The matron-hou is a tiny, wiry named Madeleine or "Madi." She through the roo day, making beds,

Dear M,D,

Just middle of Features, papers an what they It's (Peter Du idea for them. It and the p: I've last few

THIS SPACE MAY BE USED FOR WRITING

Dear two (savep$for Liz?),

It must be a bit lonely with Daddy away, or are you rather doing the town during the day? I'm driving on a ladies and an old right.

Mother's letter was waiting for me or lonely no... at on tra...

Liz came in the afternoon, so I feel caught up on the news. Paris is her most beautiful right now, and I wish we could share walks through the Luxembourg and the shopping for croissants each morning. The wonder part is just beginning, although the bits of green haven't yet begun to appear. I think it will all happen in a few weeks — that magic.

I see I'll be flooded with tourists, but no family among them. Do tell them I have to keep early nights. It will be fun to see them. Do Will Betty and Hughie cross the channel with Marguerite? They haven't seen Paris yet, and it would be a shame to miss it.

Last night I went to a friend's apartment for dinner (Grace Burpett Liz, you remember her) — Francine Miller and...

June 17, 1952

if a quickie as I'm in the
f a story for UNESCO
tion which goes to news-
s in backward areas to lift

signment. I saw the editor
suggested drafting several
val before going to work on
t encouraging project yet
by good.
st unbearably homesick the
for anything or anyone but

...e my love, Talk of gathering greens
...des me long for home. Yes, I miss
...appear so fast when you live
I've been going t the discussion
whether a ski lodge on the border
I have friends going both places
at Christmas. Do hope you
don't forget Jim + John moreley).
...xmas I'd curl up + die!

Copyright © 2014 by Beverley Lehman West

All rights reserved. Except by a reviewer, no part of this publication may
be reproduced, stored in a retrieval system, or transmitted, in any form
or by any means, electronic, mechanical, photocopying, recording, or
otherwise, without the prior written permission of the author.

Print
ISBN-10
096295571X
ISBN-13:
978-0-9629557-1-6

EBOOK
ISBN-10:
0988339668
ISBN-13:
978-0-9883396-6-8

Editor: Nancy Rekow, nancyrekow@msn.com
Design: Cliff Vancura, c.vancura@cliffvancura.com
Cover Design: Stefan Killen and Peter West
Author photo: Zuzana West Sadkova, amina@email.cz

Table of Contents

PART I

"They still sell absinthe around here, don't they?"

1952-1955

PART II

Trying to Fit In Again

1955-1963

PART III

Back to Paris with a Backpack & Hair Dye

1993-Present

Dedication

To the sailor I met on the train

You meant nothing to me at the time.
I don't even remember your name.
But I'll always remember that meeting as a stepping
stone between San Francisco and Paris,
and the rest of my life.

— from the girl in the big black coat.

Preface

How did this memoir come into being?

Some of these short pieces were inspired by writing workshops over the past 40-plus years. Others I wrote as letters home to San Francisco in the 50s. Luckily, my mother carefully saved every letter I wrote back then during those three and a half years in Paris. As you will see, this book is a collection of various pieces, plus some poems.

Why did I want to go to Paris in the first place? I'd wanted to go to Paris ever since I was nine years old—since I'd learned to visualize Paris as that magical city where they danced in the streets, whiled away hours in cafés, and scribbled masterpieces on the Left Bank.

Movies had always been a big influence for me. Just out of high school at age 18, Hollywood seduced me with *The Razor's Edge*, starring dark-eyed Tyrone Power who lived on the Left Bank and picked up mail at the American Express—and with the background lyrics: "A small café, Mam'selle." After college, the year before I went to Paris, I saw *An American in Paris,* which featured Gene Kelley and Leslie Caron dancing through the streets. Also I went to operas—*La Traviata* and *La Bohème*—set in garrets with skylights overlooking the city. Even poverty seemed to be romantic in Paris.

At age 24, when I finally actually *got* to Paris, I sat in cafés, lived in a garret (which was hard to find) and wrote stories. And yes, I picked up my mail at the American Express.

Paris fulfilled its promise for me. My three and a half years there in the 50s were filled with adventure. Even now—years later—those are memories I can always turn to.

In Paris I was never afraid—whether waiting for a bus or *métro* at night, or walking along the bank of the Seine in the dark. I felt nothing bad could happen to me in Paris.

During my Paris years I traveled to every European country, sometimes staying in youth hostels, sometimes in small hotels with women friends—called "girls" in the 50s—or my Canadian boyfriend, and often alone. Traveling became an addiction that, years later, I bequeathed to my sons: "Money means tickets."

Why did I go to Paris? I can't imagine my life if I hadn't. Eventually, I did do the other things—married late at 39, had two children just under the wire, worked on newspapers, and eventually became an ESL teacher for 35 years (next best thing to traveling). I still cross my 7s, eat with my fork in my left hand, and am never quite satisfied unless I have a croissant for breakfast. And I've never stopped writing, with Paris as my muse—in cafés, in libraries, on ferryboats, on buses—news articles, stories, poetry and, now, this book.

When my younger sister
came back from France
the first time she had clothes
and perfume that swept the house
as if she had come upon
a stolen treasure all at once.

Her face was a movie
star's, the thin line
of her eyebrows traced the delicate
script of Europe,
unreadable to us.

She could no longer find words
for common things
and uncommon emotions,
she maintained, were best left
in the original.

Excerpt from "Her Visits," by Linda Orr,
A Certain X, L'Epervier Press (1980)

Part I

"They still sell absinthe around here, don't they?"

Paris, 1952-1955

Setting Out: Love on the Coach

March, 1952

When Mother, Daddy and Liz delivered me to the railroad station in San Francisco to catch a train for the first leg of my journey to Paris, Mother whispered, "Look! There's a handsome young ensign. You should sit beside him."

I set my imitation alligator hatbox on the window seat next to the young sailor, who then helped Daddy lift my suitcase to the rack above us. He was about my age—23 or 24—about six feet tall, fairly thin, with blond hair on his wrists.

"There's still time to upgrade your ticket," Daddy said. "We can buy you a sleeper."

"No, no. I want to pay for this whole trip myself!" But I gave him an extra hug. I was traveling coach rather than Pullman, because I wanted Paris to be all mine. My $300 savings needed to last—at least till I could sell enough stories to live on.

It was March. I'd chosen that month so I could be in Paris as winter turned to romantic spring. Then Mother, Daddy and Liz would come to visit in September, if Daddy's sabbatical came through. Which, of course, it would. By that time, when they met me in Paris, I would be fluent, published—and perhaps living in a garret, as in *La Traviata*, my favorite opera. Also maybe having a secret affair with a Frenchman.

After kisses and more advice—"Don't lose your ticket; brush your hair and cream your face; don't talk to strangers." (The ensign wasn't one?)—the three of them left, and I slid across those two creased, dark blue woolen knees of his to my seat.

I remember very little about that first afternoon. We didn't say much to each other. Probably I wrote a few lines in my journal with my new fountain pen, and paged through *Mademoiselle*—the car quiet except for the rumbling wheels. Certainly didn't even put a dent in *War and Peace*, which I took on most long trips. At dinnertime, I went to the dining car ahead of the ensign and purposely sat at a table with a well-dressed older couple from Los Angeles. After all, the ensign might have overheard what Mother said, so I didn't want to look too obvious. In honor of Paris, I had red wine—from Napa Valley—with my meal.

Back in the coach it was easier to talk. Did you have the chicken? The sauce was too spicy. Yes, he agreed. Where do you live? Where are you going? To Paris? Alone?

I had a feeling he didn't approve. I couldn't imagine anyone not wanting to go to Paris—preferably alone.

Gradually the car got a little cold, so I pulled my long black wool coat over myself and snoozed about five minutes. Then it began to happen. One hand around my shoulders, the other on my knee. I removed that hand, but did put my head on his shoulder, and he seemed to be satisfied for a while. We talked a little more. How big is your family? How long have you been in the Navy? Two years. Do you like it? Then the hand went back to my knee, and I removed it with a sort of giggle. "Don't," I said.

"Why not?" I couldn't really think why not, so the next time I let it stay. He had a blond crew cut and straight teeth—was nice and clean and handsome enough, I decided. About 10 o'clock, when they turned off the lights, we stopped being quite so discreet. We kissed and catnapped and did everything two people could do without "going all the way" and—whenever we were both awake—kissed some more. He caught on and didn't try for more.

In the morning, when the lights came on, I took my hatbox along into the restroom, where I washed and changed into my white Peter Pan blouse. A brochure in the seat pocket had told us that the train had a Vista Dome from which one could view "the glorious Feather River Canyon in California, the famous Mormon Tabernacle in Salt Lake City, and the spectacular Glenwood Canyon in Colorado." But I have no memory of any vistas.

I went back to my seat. He had washed too. As our tongues met, I tasted not wine, but peppermint toothpaste.

My first passport

Ships Cross Mid-Atlantic
March, 1952

A blare from our sister Liberté.
We, Ile de France, respond,
all rush to port, to wave.

Others go to Paris 6 weeks, 6 months, a year,
but I have a one-way ticket and a typewriter.
Of course I can support myself!

Salt air whets my appetite—
bouillon and British cracker in a deck chair
then a multi-course French meal with Brie and Bordeaux.

I'm not used to either but become devoted
to everything French—
even communist riots in Paris.

Waves crash against the ship.
Many people turn green, but I am fine—
Ready now for bouillabaisse and foie gras.

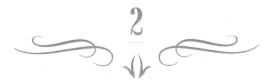

Aboard the Ile de France

March, 1952

"*Ma chère* family:
It's the fourth day at sea and I'm as indelicately full of health as ever even though almost everyone else has "*mal de mer*." I think this rough sea is just great. It makes me feel giddy.

Petit déjeuner is served from 7 to 9 a.m. and I always make it just under the wire. This morning the dining room was practically empty and those few folks who did manage to get there had a sort of green look about them. I wonder how long my own luck will last.

There's nothing more fun than being a *jeune fille* aboard a French liner—even in Tourist Class. One merely smiles and mumbles something in very high schoolish French, and doors open to Cabin and even First Class. I've swum in the pool with Cabin Class and played deck tennis (you throw a rubber loop back and forth across a net) on the outdoor top deck, which is strictly for First Class passengers and their poodles—who are usually First Class, too.

Had I known the classes were interchangeable, I would have brought evening clothes, as the lack of same is the only thing stopping me from going to the dances.

We do have dancing in the Tourist lounge too. Sort of tea dancing with a very nice little orchestra. Also movies in the evenings.

I have two cabin mates. One is an older woman—50-ish—who is French, speaks no English and refuses to slow down her French enough for me to understand her. Instead of repeating slowly, she chooses other words and utters them even faster than her original ones—so we communicate mostly by moving our hands and pointing at objects.

The other is a quiet, serious American girl my age who's a member of a Zionist organization that is working to help keep the new Jewish state of Israel afloat. She is a teacher, and is going to Israel to live. She doesn't speak a word of French, so I have to act as interpreter between my two roommates. This girl, Toby, takes her meals at the early hour—most young people eat at the late hour—and studies Hebrew most of the day. Lots of her friends came to see her off.

My table companions are great fun. Two American writers—men—one French woman whom I *can* understand sometimes, a girl who speaks both French and English, and a tall, cute French flier who was stationed in Texas. The writers are about 40—one is a freelancer who lives in Greenwich Village and the other a staff writer for a horticulture magazine. The latter is going to Athens first and following the seasons to Italy and France. I knew I'd meet writers in Paris, but didn't expect to on the boat going over!

The two Americans have tried to make dates with me and my new friend Angela—she sits at another table, but we're usually together in the evening. However we've evaded them thus far, as they're a little old for us. We have gone out with a couple of monitors, non-commissioned employees, who are young and attractive. Not really dated but have played deck tennis and gone to the movies with them. We've kept that at a minimum as we're not quite sure if it's proper since they aren't passengers. However, the general feeling with the French is "If it's fun, who cares if it's proper."

I paid 1750 francs ($5) for a deck chair, which I haven't had a spare minute or inclination to sit in yet. The fee includes a blanket. If you sit out on the deck, you get bouillon in the morning and tea and a perfectly awful crackerish cookie in the afternoon. We've been around for tea—after playing ping pong—but I've never drunk it while sitting in my deck chair.

The waves are really crashing against the ship this morning. It feels as if we're about to get shipwrecked, but I still feel fine. In fact I wish it were time for one of the two-hour meals the French are famous for. The food is wonderful and they use a lot of plates and service plates. There's always fish and meat, vegetables, soup, cheese—a small piece—and of course wine and coffee. They serve butter with the rolls occasionally and when they do it's always mentioned on the menu, *beurre*. Strange?

I'm *always* going to go Tourist Class. I met a girl at the pool who is traveling with her mother First Class and hates it. She said everyone is very formal and only three people have spoken to them since they've been aboard.

Those people I've seen up on the First Class deck just walk around with their dogs or read by themselves. They don't even talk to other people who are walking dogs. So don't go First Class!

Every night at midnight we advance our watches one hour. It's an awful hour to have to do it, as that is when everything is most exciting and gay.

Taking the French line is a good way to get acquainted with the language. The bath steward and the cabin steward speak no English so I'm forced to learn a few new phrases. I sometimes wonder if the cabin steward knows French even, for he comes cheerfully into the cabin whether I've said *"Qui est là?"* ("Who is it?") or *"Pas entrez"* ("Don't come in") to his knock. Consequently I lock the door when I'm actually dressing.

Everyone laughs and tries to assist when we Americans start murdering the language. If we get something right they are delighted and if we make a bad mistake, they clap their hands with just as much glee.

I really don't know when I've had so much fun. It's like a different life. If my trunk gets lost or someone steals my passport, I'm sure I'll feel *"n'importe."* Unless of course it keeps me from getting into Paris.

Just a few more days and I'll be there!

Continued—It's now Wednesday. Tomorrow morning we arrive in Plymouth and that evening in Le Havre. We sleep aboard that night and take the train from Le Havre to Paris in the morning. Better, I think. This is the only letter I've attempted to write. Will do the others in Paris first thing. Also will make some job contacts as my savings won't last forever.

Last night I was invited to the Captain's ball in First Class and went. It was fun and the orchestra divine. However, as they were having a costume party in Cabin Class, which also included us, Angela and I left the duller First Class party at midnight and stayed till 4 a.m. at the Cabin Class party. The orchestra played on even though they were ready to drop. Everyone had paper hats, noisemakers and threw small white balls at each other. Lots of people from First Class came down too. No, we weren't with the "monitors" as they aren't allowed at the parties. There are other interesting men aboard whom we've met lately.

The best party of all was the Tourist Class one, held night before last. Same entertainment, but the atmosphere was even more fun. Our table at dinner—eight people—plan to get together Saturday night in Paris for a party at Micheline's, my French table mate's, house.

How I love these French people. Every minute of the trip has been wonderful. I haven't missed a moment of it by being sick or oversleeping. I really hate the thought of landing.

By the way, received your letters and all the packages—waiting for me in my cabin when I arrived on board. All four Bolsters came down from Port Washington to see me off—Cousin Billy, now 11, was very excited and said he wants to be a sailor.

Today we passed the *Liberté* on its way back to New York. We saluted and so did she. I waved in case someone had field glasses. It was very close and all the passengers went up on deck to watch.

Today was smoother and most of the people felt better. You'd really hate me as I've turned into one of those people who carries on bright conversations before breakfast. I have to keep reminding myself how I've always detested those people—except my sweet little sister whom I miss most of all.

It's kind of like the first day at kindergarten. A constant state of excited anticipation. Not a sour note yet. My French is improving a little. I'll have this mailed in Plymouth tomorrow.

* * *

Continued in Paris—!— Saturday afternoon. (Didn't get this mailed in Plymouth.)

I'm now in my little room in the Hotel Madison in the Saint-Germain-des-Prés area. And from what I've seen of Paris so far, *c'est* wonderful.

The last night on shipboard they split up the Americans and French at dinner, apparently so the Americans would not see the amount the French people tip. However, most of us had gotten the straight scoop from our French friends and the amount was far less than the guide books advise. But I tipped well, considering I love the French and their food and their service.

Anyway, at my table that last night was an American man in his mid-20s who'd been a Greek guerilla during the war. He works in New York, plans to spend a week or two in Paris before going on to Greece. He was awfully attractive with big white teeth and gave me quite a rush. Went dancing with him that night. I haven't heard anything from him in Paris yet, but he was so very attentive, I was sure he'd get my address from someone. We'll see.

England looked beautiful from the ship. Green grass and red brick buildings—far different from the New York Harbor. I would have loved to get off the ship for a while but it was impossible.

French customs officials are just as awful as you've read. Luckily for me a French girl went through customs with me. On the train from Le Havre there were eight of us in one compartment with the luggage precariously placed in a rack above us. A little man in a dark blue uniform came through and said one of my bags was going to fall and would have to be put someplace else which cost me 250 francs. It also meant I'd have to go through customs at the train station instead of getting it over with on the train. Although this French girl was dead tired, she waited while I went through my extra customs inspection. I would have been most confused if she hadn't, and then we checked our bags and went to a café for lunch. It was cold and raining a little so the outside chairs, made of wicker, were not in use, though they'd optimistically been left outside. She, Claire, conversed with people and then told me in English that the weather had only been bad for two days.

We'd paid porters about 20 million times so I was not surprised when, after engaging our respective taxis, she grabbed a huge iron cart and instructed the baggage master to put the luggage on it. Then we wheeled it out to the taxis ourselves. People said things in French, which sounded like, "Will you take care of my luggage when you're through?" Anyway, I managed to get safely to the Madison and was expected there.

Another funny thing about the train is that you lower the window and scream *Porteur!* and then throw your luggage out the window onto his waiting cart.

After I got settled at the hotel, I went out for a walk in the rain. Paris is just exactly what you'd expect from the songs, books, movies and poems. They sell fish, flowers and clothes in the street. The cobblestones are easy to walk on in high heels. There are hundreds of side streets and the houses and hotels have little balcony railings on most of the windows.

The streets look as if they should be made of papier maché as part of a musical comedy setting. I really can't describe it. You three will just have to come over and see it yourselves.

It's not all perfection here—I saw a man and woman sleeping on newspapers, which they'd placed over a grate with the warm air coming up from the métro. There's a lot of poverty still, left over from World War II. And to think beautiful Paris was occupied less than 10 years ago.

My room is unbelievably small, but I rather like it. It has an iron bed and a portable closet that is too short for even street dresses to hang properly, and the room is much too small if I should be so drastic as to open my trunk. So far I've been wearing what I had on the boat.

I have a window, which looks out on a blank wall. The bath is on another floor. I took one last night and the bathroom is so small I had to inhale to close the door. Despite all this, the bath seemed luxurious.

After my short walk I returned to the hotel about 6:00, took my bath and went to bed, sleeping until 10:30 this morning. I guess the activities on shipboard were more exhausting than I thought at the time. Tonight is the party our table is having at the French girl's— Micheline's—house. It should be fun. I'm being picked up by one of the American writers.

The W.C. is very funny. When you close the door, the light goes on. That is, at night. During the day it seems to know enough not to go on.

My room has a small iron grill balcony outside the window. It's too small to sit out there, but just the right size to stand and be serenaded. No one has done that yet, though.

An odd thing has happened to me. I'm forgetting my English. I can't seem to spell or get the grammar right!

This morning I went out for a late breakfast, purchased the *New York Herald* at a paper stand, and went into a café where there were no chairs. Everyone stood and ate. I ordered *café noir* and asked for a menu. Instead the waiter brought me bread. I'm going to starve over here.

I absolutely adore being called "Mademoiselle." It really sounds so much nicer than "Miss."

Everyone around here seems about my age. Not just at the hotel but in the bookstores, of which there are many on Boulevard St. Germain.

I must try to find the American Express office now to see if I have any mail or messages.

By the way, this is a very safe city. No one has tried to pick my pocket or pick me up—worse luck!—so don't worry.

I haven't really seen a thing yet, but won't wait to mail this. Will describe more in my next letter. However I do know I love Paris.

And I love you too,
Bevs

Tennis on the top deck

My First Bidet
March, 1952

Voila—my first bidet—
aboard the Ile de France—
white, ceramic, almost like an American toilet
but shallow.

Suzette explains:
"You turn the tap
and the water
swirls around.
You wash yourself every time you pee."
She reddens:
"I put on a little perfume."

"Then what?" I ask.

"My husband says,
when he throws me down on the bed
on a Saturday afternoon,

'Suzette, it's always so sweet
I could kiss it.'"

I'm only twenty-four
but I know
I will certainly marry a Frenchman.

Hotel Madison: They Wouldn't "Changez le Lit"

March, 1952

The maid didn't understand. So I double-checked my pocket dictionary. Yes, bed was "*le lit.*" Then I asked at the desk, would they please "*changez le lit?*" I'd been staying at the Hotel Madison, a block from St.-Germain-des-Prés, for two weeks, and the sheets had never been changed.

The tall, thin woman at the desk was one of three sisters who owned and managed the hotel. Cheerful, businesslike, they all wore sensible, low-heeled shoes. Most un-Parisian, I thought. She hesitated, then said, "*Oui, Mademoiselle.*" Then I walked across the bridge in the fog to the American Express at the Place de l'Opéra where I could wait in line to pick up my mail from the clerk, and meanwhile speak a little English, which made me feel less lonely. Sometimes there'd be someone in the mail line that I'd met on the boat or at coffee after the American Church service.

This time at the American Express I did run into someone, but it was an American woman, my mother's age, who said, "I can always tell our girls. They're so fresh and clean."

Her eyes took in my Peter Pan collar. I wished I'd pushed it under the neck of my pale blue Hadley pullover. I wanted to blend in, to be French. I must buy something dark, at least darker than baby blue. Maybe a black turtleneck sweater, like the existentialists.

The American lady was about five foot two, wore white gloves and a veil, and reminded me a little of Mother whom I was missing already, though I'd been trying for years to get away from her. Now

I had five months on my own, before my parents and sister arrived, to work on my French.

There were three letters for me at the American Express: one each from Liz and Mother and one from Barbara Ann, an American I'd met on the boat, but had lost track of. She was from Chicago, had worked for the railroad there, and had saved enough for four months travel in Europe. She wrote that she was in a pension at Place St. Sulpice and wanted me to see it.

"I know you're working on your French, and everybody here speaks it. You'd pick it up fast. Myself, I'm off to Italy. But let's keep in touch." I'd certainly look into that pension.

Now it was starting to rain so I decided to take a bus back to the hotel. I climbed up, paid my fare, and moved to the back where I could see better. I watched the waiters in cafés putting up the awnings and glass partitions for evening customers who'd come in for *apéritifs*. I watched last-minute shoppers and children coming home from school. Then before the bus had crossed the Seine, the rain stopped and the sun came out again, so I decided to get out in the fresh air and walk the rest of the way. Suddenly, it didn't matter whether or not they'd *ever* change the sheets.

However, when I got to my room, two workmen in dark blue cotton shirts and pants had just moved the bed to the other side of the small room.

"*Changez le lit*" I thought. ("Change the bed.")

"*Non, non, Monsieur!*" I pulled out the corner of the linen sheet to show what I meant.

"*Changez ça, s'il vous plaît.*" ("Change that, please.")

"*Oui, madame.*" They looked at each other. The taller one scratched his head as they walked out.

I checked the dictionary again. Although "bed" was "*lit*," to change the sheets was "*faire les draps.*"

"*Changez le lit*" indeed. I would have to work on my French!

Baden-Baden: Mud Baths & Reading at a Casino

Spring, 1952

"Over here, Bev. Here we are!"

I looked around, followed the American voice above the German babble. There they were: my college friend Jane, with her short, curly brown hair and shining glasses, beside a small, smiling woman who must be her American roommate in Bremen, Germany—also a Jane.

They'd been waiting for me at the railroad station in Baden-Baden, where we planned to spend a three-day weekend sightseeing. And certainly, now that I understood Baden meant "bath," we would take the mineral baths, also called the "Kur" (cure). Europeans took the baths for arthritis, rheumatism, and all manner of aches and pains, but we, in our indomitable 20s, took them just for fun as part of the *grande expérience*.

"Good. You've only got one bag," Jane McTavish, my college chum, said.

"Of course. I always travel light." I didn't tell her about the things left on my Paris bed: a travel iron, a typewriter, two extra pairs of shoes and my black scoop-neck dress. Better to let her think I was a seasoned traveler.

In three months, this was my first trip outside the country. French law required that tourists have their passports stamped every three months. Those who remained in France beyond that time were required to pay many French francs for a *carte d'identité*. To avoid this, I was taking a little trip across the border. But already such a

Francophile, I'd had to drag myself away from Paris.

"Let's go to the beer garden for a bite before we go to the hotel," she said.

"*Wunderbar!*" I used one of my three German words.

Jane led us to an outdoor café that featured black and green tables and green umbrellas. "We don't need a menu," the second Jane said, and they both giggled. I soon learned why. They talked briefly with the waiter and he almost immediately reappeared with a large brass tray holding three cups of coffee, a pitcher of cream and three huge slices of chocolate cake covered with heavy cream (*mit schlag*).

"Wait! Let me get a picture of this!" I fished my camera out of my purse. Then the waiter returned and said,

"I take you together." I still have that snapshot—cake, *schlag* and grins. We ordered second slices, finishing every crumb. "Well, now we can work it off in the baths," said the second Jane.

In a place called Baden-Baden, you have to have a *baden*, so we left my suitcase with the waiter-photographer in the beer garden and headed for the baths—spacious, immaculate, and just a short walk away. There a sturdy blonde woman smeared mud all over me and wiped it off with fragrant wet pine shavings. Then we went to the pools. After five minutes hiding behind towels, I lost all modesty and simply gave myself to it. Several cool pools. Then immersion in hot spring water. Then a nap.

Later, we picked up my suitcase from the beer garden and took it to the hotel. From the two Janes, I learned a travel tip—an easy one in those days of youthful bladders: don't waste money on a room with a private bath. So we didn't. In our room we decided to change for dinner and, while it was still light, walk around the town.

Jane McTavish had gotten her job as information clerk for the State Department while still in the U.S. As a Journalism major at the University of Nevada, I'd been offered one too. But I had one stipulation—my job had to be in Paris, where they danced in the streets like a continuous Gene Kelley movie. Not in serious Germany where wartime rubble, which I'd seen in *The March of Time* newsreels, was still lying around, waiting to be cleaned up.

So Jane had her way paid to Bremen while I, because I'd specified Paris, went on my own—with money from the sale of my Chevy—to Paris.

At that time, in 1952, the thick Black Forest was still lush and unpolluted, so we walked and picnicked on bread, beer and sausages as if it would all be there forever. The next two days we spent taking mineral baths at the *baden* we'd found that first day, and visiting a plush casino a taxi ride from the hotel. At the casino, men in black knickers, black velvet shoes and white stockings dashed from table to table, emptying ashtrays for well-to-do Germans and a few French tourists.

One of the brochures told us that the mirrored casino had been inspired by the Versailles Palace. But I was a little disappointed in the atmosphere. There was none of that feverish excitement I remembered from my college days in the casinos of Reno. In fact, I'd brought along *The Magic Mountain* to read while sitting on a bench waiting for the Janes to play a card game each. But an important-looking man in a black suit frowned at me. It was a lively part of the book, with the Russian couple running around naked, so I hid it under my jacket to read surreptitiously. Finally the manager came over with a pointed "ahem," and shamed me into putting the book away and to wait outside for my friends.

Well, not everyone can boast of being thrown out of a famous casino for reading.

* * *

The next day I climbed on the train back to Paris. A woman, probably Swiss, pulled open the compartment door, stepped in and found a seat across from me. She was slim, well-exercised, and dressed conservatively in a tan linen suit. She opened her suitcase, pulled out a fold-over packet of stationary, slid out a white sheet, balanced it on the suitcase, and began to write.

From across the aisle, I sipped my paper cup of coffee and watched her. No doubt she'd been staying with a friend, I decided, so this must be a bread and butter letter. She wrote the entire page without stopping, without rereading a single sentence to see if a word was misspelled or if she'd left anything out.

When finished, she folded it twice like a square handkerchief, then put it in a square envelope, which she addressed, lick-sealed, stamped, and slipped neatly into her purse with a half-smile. She probably does crossword puzzles in ink, I thought, wishing I had the nerve to spill coffee on her tan skirt.

Bev, Jane & Jane McTavish with cake & *schlag* in Baden-Baden

Flower Market and the Hotel de Ville

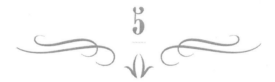

On Henri's Vespa: With Kisses

April, 1952

I remember lying half-naked on—and sometimes in—a bed and still not "doing it." But we did a lot of kissing back in the 50s.

So my date with tall, curly-haired Henri, whom I'd met through Betty Southard, a classmate at the Alliance Française, was not especially unusual. He gave me a whirlwind tour of Paris monuments, lighted up and seen from the back of his Vespa, and we kissed whenever either of us felt like it. We'd eaten dinner at a jammed student restaurant on the Boulevard St. Michel, then had coffee, costing more than the dinner, at the Deux Magots, and now came the best part—riding on the back of his blue Vespa with wind pulling at my hair.

I wrapped my arms tight around Henri's waist, hands safely on his brass belt buckle.

"*Ça va?* You OK?" he'd turn and ask. "Going too fast? Shall we stop?"

We did stop. And often. At his suggestion or mine, standing at the lighted Madeleine, or Louvre or *Arc de Triomph*. At night the grey buildings of Paris lit up magically—romantic enough for a little lovemaking in front of each one.

"I'm getting cold, Henri. Can we stop at my hotel? It's just over the Pont Neuf. I'll get a coat."

"Of course, *chérie*." Another kiss and he whisked me off to the Madison at St.-Germain-des-Prés. He parked in front of the building and locked his Vespa. We ignored the elevator and cuddled all the way up the four flights. I unlocked the door with my brass key and turned on the low reading lamp so we could see our way in.

We lay on the bed for a few minutes and kissed. He switched off the lamp and began pulling my brown pullover sweater up, off my shoulders. "No, Henri! Leave my sweater alone." I kissed him again, on the mouth and neck and ear, but tried to push his hand away from my breast and sweater. That was getting dangerous.

"Stop!" I said. "You can't take off my sweater. No! No! You'll have to go!"

"What?" he said. "I don't believe this!"

"Go, Henri." I pushed him away and got off the bed. "You have to go NOW."

"*Mais, chérie.* Why?" I opened the door and pointed to the hall. He stomped off, red-faced, slamming the door. Then came a clang on the wrought-iron elevator door.

The next day I started telling brown-eyed Betty what had happened. But an amazed Henri had already told her. "Beverley's a virgin," Betty had explained to him.

"Impossible. She's over 20! You Americans are strange."

But he could hold up his head again—his French manhood restored.

6

Ana, The Maid

May, 1952

I hurried to climb the steep flight of stairs to my new room at Madame Dessart's pension because the *minuterie* (time switch) in the narrow stairwell allowed me only one minute until the light went out. There was the start of a short story in my notebook still to type up. I'd written it over a *café crème* at a small round marble table in the Select, just as those writers did in the 20s. Everyone said it would be easy to write in Paris, and it was. Even the *garçon* in his long starched apron helped by never hovering, so I was able to sit and write as long as I felt like it.

I did beat the *minuterie* up the stairs and opened the door. The room was flooded with afternoon light from the two windows above rue Honoré-Chevalier.

"Elle ne part pas," (It won't come out,) a woman's voice said sadly.

It was Ana, the small bony maid, scrubbing hard with her brush on the linoleum floor under the washbasin. She sat on the floor, a bare knee on each side of her brush and bucket, and looked up to talk to me as if this were a completely natural position. Her light brown hair was pinned back tightly. She'd folded the portable bamboo-legged *bidet* against the wall to give her more room. She pointed to the stain, which looked like coffee and could have been.

Every morning, Ana and another maid, pretty plump Marie, brought breakfast—coffee, milk, two pieces of French bread and two small packets of butter—on trays up the stairs to me and my roommate, Joan. Marie often got into trouble with Madame Dessart for sleeping with the young men pensioners. Early one morning when I walked down the hall to the toilet, I heard Madame chastising Marie loudly, *"Tu es toujours en retard!"* (You are always late!) But Ana was never late.

"Ça ne fait rien," (That doesn't matter,) I told Ana.

She continued scrubbing anyway, adding water from her bucket to a powder that looked and smelled as if it would scrub anything out. I wished she would finish and leave, not because of the smell of the powder or because I wanted to type up my story, but because I felt uncomfortable standing there, looking down at her. It was postwar France and the American dollar could buy almost anything. She, a woman about my age, was poor. But I couldn't change the situation. Ana wasn't going to stand up, or go to school, or change her life.

Hi, Frenchie: Schiaparelli & Paquin Fashion Shows

June, 1952

If you sit at the Café de la Paix for an hour or so, you're supposed to see someone you know. And I usually did—though it might just be a fellow passenger from the Ile de France.

I'd been to the American Express where I stood in a long line to get my mail. Then I sat at the large umbrella-filled terrace of the Café de la Paix to read and reread the five-page letter from Liz, who'd be coming over to Paris at the end of the summer. Finally I put it back in the envelope and looked up to see an American soldier smiling at me from the next table. Clean-cut and blond, with high cheekbones and a strong nose, he looked a lot like Bill Keller, a childhood friend who'd lived up the street in San Francisco.

"Can I sit with you?" he asked.

"Of course." It would be good to speak English for a while.

Oliver seemed pleasant and quiet. I let him pay for my coffee when he paid for his three or four beers. He walked with me along the broad, sunny Champs Elysées, looking in the shop windows. Though I loved clothes, none of the spring blouses and jackets in the windows tempted me. Being in Paris was enough. I'd never been out with a soldier before, if you'd call this going out. Which I wouldn't.

"Here, I'll buy you a set of postcards. Which do you want?" His beery breath was too close to my face. I hoped he wouldn't try to kiss me. We stopped at a large, round kiosk, where a stocky man in a black beret rearranged the postcards and the magazines—the *Figaro*, *Paris Soir*, *Elle*, the *Paris Herald-Tribune*, and the weekly *Spectacle* with its listings of movies, plays and art shows.

The postcards were bright, garish pictures of the Eiffel Tower and Notre Dame and other standard attractions. They were in spiral packets so you could tear one off to mail. I didn't want any, but I didn't say so. If they hadn't been quite so shiny, I could have sent them—maybe—to someone. I think, after many years, I still have the packet he bought me that day, in the blue Paris box on the top shelf of my closet.

"Let's take a cab. I just got paid," he said.

"OK, but I have to go back in half an hour. I have an appointment."

I felt safe with the driver there—three in a cab. But how awful if Oliver tried to kiss me with his smelly breath! "Hi Frenchie," he yelled drunkenly out the back window of our taxi. The Frenchman on the street raised his eyebrows. I cringed and pretended I wasn't there.

I could ask to be let out at the American library, which had a tempting fireplace where I liked to read and smoke Gitanes—France was such a civilized place. After I got out of the cab I'd go into the library. Oliver would never follow me there.

"My time's up, Oliver," I said and asked the driver in French to let me out at the intersection near the Pont Neuf and the library. I knew Oliver didn't know French so couldn't contradict me. The last I saw of him was a droopy-eyed person in olive drab, looking out of a black taxi.

After that Oliver encounter, I certainly didn't feel inspired to write. But I had two story ideas that an editor—Waldo Wallis of John MacNair's *European News Service*, whom I'd met through a connection at the American Church—had said he was interested in. One was about a fashion show at Schiaparelli where I was to go that afternoon. I'd arranged to meet an American friend there from the Ile de France—Jeanmarie Meiser, who wanted to see it too.

Everything was supposed to be perfect in Paris and I insisted to myself that it was. I didn't see the rudeness—ever—in the French. But now as I look back, there was a lot of it if you weren't actually in the process of buying something. The French were still suffering from the war and naturally they resented the "haves."

Jeanmarie was waiting at the library, métro map in hand. She was tall and thin and, in her black print dress and matching jacket, looked like a model. I regretted those *croissants* with marmalade and butter I'd had that morning and the *omelette au jambon* I'd eaten with crusty French bread for lunch. But who could resist French cooking? Certainly not me. At least I hadn't had any dessert.

The fashion show was exciting. Although we didn't have invitations, we simply walked into Schiaparelli's and said we'd love to be allowed to see the new styles. I mentioned I was going to write an article about it. They were awfully nice to us, gave us engraved invitations—actually just printed to look engraved—for the Schiaparelli show, and also for one the next day at Paquin's on the rue de la Paix.

We sat on spindly, cushioned chairs against the white enameled walls of a room with high ceilings. About six young women—my 1952 notes called them "girls"—sauntered down the runway in elaborate outfits of silk shantung with small hats hiding all their hair. There were lots of checks, large and small, worn together, and accessories were bright: hats, gloves and belts of cerise and chartreuse.

The next day, at Paquin's, I saw that push-up sleeves were in style, and that Liz's white jacket, which I'd borrowed, was right in fashion, as was my own blue rayon duster. The models at both houses had a sort of empty look in their faces. Some of them looked hard and others looked rather dull and bored with living—even in Paris.

Jeanmarie said, "I think we've seen enough fashion shows."

"Yes," I told her. "It cuts into your afternoon."

We walked out into dusky rue de la Paix, off Boulevard des Capucines. Paris was still warm and the waiters were setting terrace tables for another evening of stimulating café conversations, drinks, laughter…and 15% *service compris* tips.

Le Tabou: Dancing in a Cave & Visiting Les Halles

Spring, 1952

"You'll need your jacket. Remember we're going down into a *cave*," my adventurous English roommate, Joan, said. We were about to leave Madame Dessart's pension with two French boys who also lived there: tall, dark-haired Jacques, Joan's current boyfriend, and Gabriel, who studied architecture at the Sorbonne.

I knew about *caves*—dark, dank places where you walked down slippery steps, trying not to touch the wet stone walls. I'd been to an art show in one, listened to the clarinet of Claude Luter in another, and American jazz clarinetist Sidney Bechet in a third—the Vieux-Colombier. But this would be my first visit to the wild and spontaneous Tabou on rue Dauphine, home of the existentialists.

I was dressed for it: black turtleneck sweater, black pants and then a jacket—black of course—in the style of Juliette Gréco, a spokesperson of existentialism with her low-pitched voice singing such songs as "Feuilles Mortes" (Dead Leaves). As we left, I viewed myself in the pension window, not without some pride. "I look like a depraved Sartre follower," I said.

But Joan giggled, "Not with your round face and freckles." She was enviably thin, though I knew she didn't consider that an asset. The grass is always greener I decided, taking a deep breath and holding in my stomach.

We walked down rue Honoré-Chevalier, past the sand-colored stone church, St. Sulpice, that marked our neighborhood. A famous monument, it was lighted with powerful floodlights and couples strolled by the fountain or sat on stone benches out in the church courtyard in the sweet warm air.

At the Tabou, we edged carefully down into a musty room, as guitar jazz wafted up the stairs. It was decorated that night with a "fatal apple" motif—cloth apples and green paper leaves hung on the walls and ceiling.

Some dancers' faces were familiar from one of my favorite cafés—the Deux Magots in St.-Germain-des-Prés, where I liked to drink coffee and write stories in my notebook. There they'd display charcoal sketches from their portfolios, almost as big as they were, to the tourist patrons. Now I watched them dancing on the Tabou floor, sliding under their partners' legs till they were stooped and limp from fatigue.

"Look at her, over there by the bar," I said to Joan. "Now I know how they can go on."

We watched one short dancer drag herself up to the bar, where the bartender handed her a small, white pill. She put it on her tongue, swallowed a clear drink, and danced off. Several others kept doing the same thing. "That's Benzedrine, a real upper," said Jacques, who'd come north from Avignon and had lived in Paris for three years.

We jitterbugged and two-stepped until the lights went on, then sat at small tables around the stage. A marionette opera singer, about four feet tall and dressed in a green lace gown exposing an immense bosom, was the main attraction. Her bosom was attached to strings and—to laughing and clapping from the audience—one breast or the other was suddenly raised by the puppeteer whenever she hit a high note.

Once out of the dank Tabou, I took off my jacket, pulled up my sleeves and let the soft air cool my face and arms. We hailed a black Citroën taxi. *"Les Halles*, please," Jacques told the driver in French. "It's on the...."

"Je sais bien" (I know), the elderly driver shrugged. "All the tourists go there at this hour," he told us. He sped along, honking at slow cars in the intersections.

"Voilà, les Halles." The driver opened our passenger door. Jacques paid him and he looked at the coins in his hand. *"Merci, bien,"* he said evenly, so I knew we hadn't tipped him too little or too much—something I always worried about. Too little was unacceptable and too much would make us seem like crass tourists—but of course Jacques, a Frenchman, would know.

We watched preparations for that morning's market in the 14 gray iron pavilions. Men in soiled blue shirts and pants arranged fresh apples, pears, and melons, along with carrots, turnips, leeks and cabbages, in mounds on stands. Poultry and fish in wicker baskets; meat, cheese, butter and milk—each had its own pavilion behind glass panes.

We stood at the zinc bar in *Le Pied de Cochon* (The Pig's Foot) on rue Coquillère and spooned the thick rich *soupe à l'oignon* (onion soup), which had been cooked with slices of crusty French bread and grated cheese. Even inside, we smelled the parsley, celery and carrots fighting with the scents of Provence: bouquets of garlic, thyme and laurel.

Back then we—and all Paris—assumed the market would be there forever. But, because its narrow streets were unsuitable for modern trucks, in 1969 it was moved to Rungis, south of Paris. At that, some said Paris had lost its soul.

"It was a place of bliss...the last vision of natural life in the City. It is now Paradise Lost," wrote sculptor Raymond Mason. Paris poet Louis Chevalier said, "The death of *Les Halles* has tolled the knell of Paris."

In 1979 that picturesque central market became the *Forum des Halles*—the largest pedestrian center in Europe—with 240 shops. And the bowels of *Les Halles* were converted to a huge new central *métro* and RER (*réseau express régional*) station, the largest one in the capital.

But in 1952 we ate the aromatic onion soup and drank Beaujolais amidst the fruits and vegetables shining from a recent afternoon shower. Blood-stained butchers and muscular vegetable vendors hoisted heavy crates, seemingly oblivious to the bare-shouldered night clubbers wandering about laughing, drinking, getting in their way. They also seemed oblivious to me—the quiet, black-clad, pretend existentialist.

American girl, Dutch boyfriend, French baguette

Following the French: Trip to Ibiza

June & July, 1952

Joan and I were walking near the great stone fountain at
the Place St. Sulpice across from the church—my new
neighborhood since taking Barbara Ann's advice and moving to the
French pension. We watched several Parisian children, dark-haired
and angular, leaning over to push their small boats through the
water. Usually there were dozens of children, with parents or *au
pairs*, vying for a few inches of the water.

"I ask a question in French and get an answer in English—even
when I wear my beret," I grumbled. It was July, 1952, and I'd been
working hard to get fluent ever since I'd arrived in Paris several
months before.

"I know," Joan sympathized, "but what do you expect in
summer? No self-respecting Frenchman stays in Paris."

It didn't matter so much to Joan, a Londoner who worked
for a small British travel agency—Treasure Tours—at the Place
de l'Opéra. She used French all the time in her job. But for me,
one of the main reasons for being in France was to improve my
French. How else could I qualify for being an expatriate writer, à la
Hemingway?

We walked on the cobblestoned rue Honoré-Chevalier, I
maneuvering my red lizard platform shoes along the higher parts
of the stones. These were my favorite shoes. Back then you could
wear reptile shoes without fear of raised eyebrows or a lecture from a
stranger.

On a sunny day we often ordered packed lunches from Madame Dessart's pension and ate them in the nearby Luxembourg Gardens. "I'll treat us to chairs," I said, handing a featherweight two-franc coin to a bent, elderly woman. She took a cloth from her pocket and brushed off two dusty, green metal chairs, then moved them one at a time, with some effort, to a cool spot on the gravel under a leafy tree.

"*Voilà!*" she said, eyes shining. Even at 24, I knew better than to offer help.

Four or five older men were playing *boules*, rolling a large, heavy ball similar to our bowling ball. Every few rolls, they took turns raking the gravel. I guessed they were retired or out of work.

"Oh good. Yogurt and an apple," said trim Joan. I hoped for more as I broke the string on my cardboard box, and there was. I pulled out a sandwich, a thin slice of Gruyère on a buttered baguette. Although I loved French food, the French didn't understand sandwiches, which I felt should have more inside. Crunchy lettuce and mayonnaise, at least.

"That '*voilà*' is probably the only French I'll hear all day. Except of course at the pension," I said. I'd moved to Madame Dessart's so I could practice my French with the students who lived there and with the workers from nearby factories who came there for meals.

"Well, it's not as if you're not trying," she said. "You saw *Jules and Jim* three times. And remember those gruesome plays at Le Grand-Guinòl? We both picked up a lot of *argo* (slang) that night."

I shuddered, recalling that evening at 20 bis, rue Chaptal and the ketchuppy handkerchief with a pretend severed finger in it. But linguistically, it had been a good learning experience—the actors had enunciated clearly as they shot or stabbed one another. One play was *Les Salauds vont en Enfer* or "The Bastards go to Hell" and the other, equally bloody, was *Un Coup de Fusible* or "A Gunshot."

"But you're right," Joan stirred her pension-made yogurt in the glass jar which, in the pre-recycling 50s, she would later drop in a garbage can. "I had a coffee at the Deux Magots Thursday and the only people speaking French were the waiters."

"I guess I could fall asleep listening to my Asymil records and tapes," I said. "But it's not the same thing. The lessons aren't real."

"I say, I've got it!" Joan sounded more British—even a little Cockney—when she got excited. "Take a tour, with French students, going to the Balearic Islands," she said. "The tours are cheap. They leave every two weeks."

I'd heard about those snorkeling trips. A couple of students at the pension were always showing pictures at the long table during dinner. Thin tropical fish, flat and bright as a primitive painting. I loved to swim. And I'd be speaking French. What a wonderful idea. That started me out on my great adventure of budget traveling—the thrifty French were the ones to copy.

I bought my ticket at a travel agency on Boulevard St. Michel near the *Panthéon*. Famous writers, such as Emile Zola and Saint-Exupéry, were buried in that great domed structure—another good omen for my own writing, I figured.

It was a package deal, including train fare from Paris to Barcelona, then two weeks of hotel accommodations and meals in Ibiza, a then-unknown island near Majorca. Snorkeling equipment was supposed to be included but, as it turned out, there was never quite enough to go around. So we ended up taking turns.

I told Madame Dessart I'd be away on vacation for a few weeks so she could rent out my half of the room. I left some of my clothes hanging in an armoire and kept the skeleton key, a selfish act I was to hear about when I got back. Although I thought I was a soft-spoken, polite Californian, I guess there was something of the Ugly American in me.

A maid at the pension packed me a box lunch for the train trip and I took a bus with an open back to the Gare d'Austerlitz. I stood at the end of the bus, suitcases at my feet, looking out at the shops and monuments of Paris. I could never get enough of it. Even now, more than a half-century later, I still can't. Fortunately, Paris still has some open-air buses and the buildings are as ornate as ever, although whiter. In the 50s, the buildings were soot gray and most people thought the effect would be ruined if they were cleaned.

I boarded the train with a little too much luggage but—being plump and pretty and young—I could always find someone to carry it on and stow it in the rack above:

"Je peux vous aider, Mademoiselle?" (Can I help you?)

"Oui, Monsieur, merci."

Everything about travel was fun, even a third-class train compartment on a hot summer day. And, of course, I got to use my French with conductors, porters, and compartment-mates. I was completely unembarrassed and talked to everybody. Three of the passengers were going on my tour and we played French bridge.

Meeting my tour companions across the border in Barcelona, I realized Joan had been right. I began hearing endless streams of French. Years later, I still remember phrases from those two weeks. We changed trains a couple of times. Hot! Traveling through Spain in a cashmere sweater. Smoky mountains and blue, blue sea from the windows—inviting.

Barcelona was a giant station. My companions speaking French, and I just trying to keep up. From the cool of the station, I could see horse carts and a street car. Warm, rumpled people walking slowly. Walking outside I saw policemen standing on every corner in this Franco country. As a tourist I felt detached, yet uncomfortable for the residents. Would you be afraid to talk? To buy a magazine? To go into certain buildings?

Back to my "French lessons." Angélique, a doctor's wife from Brouges, took me window-shopping in downtown Barcelona and instructed me in some nuances of the French language. She pointed at a fitted suitcase: "You're supposed to say, *'C'est complet, n'est-ce pas?'*

"And," she said in French, "Look at that painted pottery. One says it's *'typique du pays'* (typical of the country)." I repeated the phrases, knowing it was good for my French to be able to use those words with perfect pronunciation, copied from elegant Angélique. It didn't matter how unoriginal my conversation would turn out to be.

Once I saw Angélique staring at a large shop window filled with sweater sets, a coat, leather bag, high-heeled shoes, and a table of varied jewelry. She was silent. "What do you want?" I asked.

"*Un millionaire.*" A beautiful doctor's wife, she sounded as petulant as Emma Bovary.

Next day, we crowded onto an old, old passenger boat to sail to Ibiza. The kindest woman in the world lent me a washbasin she carried in her suitcase. Then a bus to tiny San Antonio and Hotel Tropical, all white with hanging knotted strings for a door. My roommate was a French woman, Genevieve. Why had I brought a travel iron? (No outlets.)

We looked around for showers: *"La douche, s'il vous plait?"* A mixture of Spanish and French from waiters and a desk clerk let us know we were to climb a flight of stairs to the roof. There, we turned on the water spigot for our first Ibizan shower. The cold water was refreshing, fortunately, as we were not to see or feel hot water for the next two weeks.

The second day on Ibiza we took a fishing boat to another island—tiny, without a single tree. Explored underwater life with *des palmes* (flippers) and *lunettes* (goggles). So many flat fish that one usually sees behind glass in aquariums. After lunch the dirty dishes were piled in the boat for the flies and we siesta'd a bit. Then sailed to a sandy beach with curling, grey-trunked trees.

The French and Spanish seemed to have little regard for human life. None of our extensive water rules. Swimming alone in strange waters, I had a feeling that if lost I'd not be missed for at least two days. I decided it was the cruelty—the intense sun, the hard blue water, the rough bare islands—that was so intriguing. And then the strange softening at sunset. The bright blue became rose and gray and the red sun set so rapidly I didn't dare look away for fear of missing it. The rocks and roads were a golden color especially at sunset. It was like the shade of the natives' skin.

Everything was so primitive—horses running in circles to thrash the wheat—or corn? Women walking slowly with buckets of water on their heads and carrying meal fixings. Our French "colony" celebrated the 14th of July—Bastille Day—with a bang-up party and strong Spanish punch topped with slices of apple and banana. I drank one and a half and was almost *ivre* (drunk). Another drink they offered was Pernod and sugar, with water slowly dripping through a pin prick in a glass saucer. After it passed, the saucer was discarded and the delicacy, in a large goblet, was ready.

Did people there really think? No one carried a book or newspaper, and the natives conversed so little. Who won the Republican nomination for president? Funny thing was it made no difference. I could have asked some tourists who arrived later, but why bother? (It was of course, Dwight Eisenhower of "I like Ike" fame—who was to have a landslide victory resulting in the Republicans gaining control of both houses.)

Our afternoon routine included a two-hour siesta: first we'd sleep, then groggily I'd write a few sentences in my journal. We'd walk off to a beach to swim, peer through leaky goggles at plants and tropical fish, then allow nature to dry us off. As there was a shortage of plastic flippers, the men got them most of the time, a fact of life I accepted back in those days. Angélique's doctor husband walked, swinging his flippers, never thinking to share. Anyway, my motive was to practice my French.

Sometimes we took out a little blue sailboat, monitored by an

Ibizan employee of the hotel. Even though, as a San Franciscan, I'd lived with a bay at my feet, I'd never learned to sail—so the little bit I learned in Ibiza was exciting. We sailed to small coves or various beaches for swimming and snorkeling, and once took a boat to the island of Fomentera for breakfast and swimming. Lunch and dinner at the hotel on Ibiza always involved several servings of rather dry goat cheese and goat meat, so even that day on Fomentera, it wasn't any surprise to be served it. Fortunately I liked it and, to this day I still buy goat cheese.

One of the monitors, Leonardo, about 18, was slight and childlike with crooked teeth. Off season he helped his father and brother carve tiny beads from pale wood into bracelets. He had a very small mouth, like a chipmunk, that watered at the corners when he spoke.

Occasionally our group would go into town to wander the narrow streets and slanted stone stairways—speaking French even there in Spain. On Sundays the local women dressed in long black shawls. All, of course, were Catholic. Masses were at 6, 8, 10 and 12.

There was another big fete day—*Fête de Mari*—with scores of sail and motorboats covered with flags. Fireworks at night and everybody out to watch. Many of the boats were overcrowded with natives and tourists. Religious symbols on the bows. A man in an impressive black robe threw a bouquet of flowers into the sea. Everybody clapped so I did too.

On Fomentera in the little village of Salina we had breakfast in a small café. Some sticky cream placed in tall glasses and freshly ground coffee poured over it. And the usual floury, tasteless Spanish bread. We swam in the very salty water. Around the edges of Salina, there were flat pools with low, stone walls to make or filter salt—evidently the town's main industry.

The other monitor, Juanito, had short, curly hair, a mouth half open all the time, spoke no French at all and didn't even try to follow the conversation. After his swim, he kept on his clinging wool trunks and scratched himself as he guided the boat with the tiller. The other Spaniards too seemed to think nothing of indiscriminate scratching, regardless of offending delicate little American tourists. Actually, I suppose since it was natural it shouldn't have bothered me.

In town, I noticed all Spanish women were fat and didn't wear girdles. Life was arranged to make them so. Restaurants and dining rooms were cool and shaded—so pleasant that one kept ordering more in order to stay—and then on a full stomach, the siesta. At least 45 minutes required after lunch. Otherwise one was no good the rest of the day.

Was I the only American left? I'd gotten sick of British accents and *ennuyer* (tired) of speaking French. Mama! In the evenings, I'd change to a cream silk sleeveless dress and high-heeled sandals for the cocktail hour and dinner on the hotel terrace—still part of my self-styled language lab.

Some of the tourists in our group planned to spend time in other parts of Spain after the Balearic Islands; others were going to youth hostels along the Riviera. I hadn't thought of anything beyond Ibiza, but those ideas intrigued me. So I ended up going to a hotel in Barcelona for a few days, and then youth-hostelling by train to exciting places in the south of France—Perpignan, Avignon, Nice, Cannes, and the perfume town of Arles.

I always traveled with my French phrase book to practice with anyone I could find to talk to. So, some weeks later I returned to Paris, sunburned and happy, with several hundred new words to enrich my vocabulary. Madame Dessart welcomed me back with a kiss on each cheek, obviously relieved the armoire key wasn't lost forever.

47 SPECTACLES DE PARIS

THEATRES - MUSIC-HALLS - CHANSONNIERS - CIRQUES

*

318   Semaine du 21 au 27 Juin 1954

A.B.C.
11, boulevard Poissonnière - Cen 10 ..
Georges ...

AMB...

Mort

DIX-HEURES
36, boulevard de Clichy - Mon. 07-48
Nouveau spectacle
Faux Pacifiés
Bouquet des œuvres printanières de
Pierre Destailles, Philippe Olive, Oléo,
Maurice Horgues, Anne-Marie Carrière,
Bernard Lavalette, Charles Bernard,
Jean Patrick et Jean Valmence,
Claude Rolland, Jean Breton,
Jean Touchard.

EDOUARD-VII
10, place Edouard-VII - Opé. 67-90

Clôture annuelle

ETOILE
35, avenue de Wagram - Gal. 84-49

Compagnie des
" Ballets de l'Etoile "

Tous les soirs à 21 h., sauf lundi.
Mat. dimanche à 15 heures.

EUROPEEN
Jusqu'au 24 juin

Récital intégral de

Charles Trenet

14 représentations exceptionnelles
Tous les soirs à 21 h., sauf mardi.
Mat. dimanche à 15 heures.

FONTAINE
10, rue Fontaine - Tri. 74-40

Clôture annuelle

GAITE-LYRIQUE
Square des Arts-et-Métiers - Arc. 63-82

Clôture annuelle

GRAND-GUIGNOL
20 bis, rue Chaptal - Tri. 28-34
Les salauds vont en Enfer
2 actes et 7 tableaux de Frédéric Dard.
Mise en scène de Robert Hossein
Un coup de fusible
de Raymond Souplex
Tous les soirs à 21 h., sauf mardi.
Mat. dimanche à 15 heures.

...AMONT
...ramont - Ric. 62-61

...thenaïs
...heur des autres
...ctes de Robert Favart
...cène de l'auteur
... Michel Sonkin
... Suzet-Maïs
... à 21 h., sauf lundi.
...che à 15 heures.

...MNASE
...n : Paule Rolle
...-Nouvelle - Pro. 16-15

Clôture annuelle

Un coup de fusible
de Raymond Souplex
Tous les soirs à 21 h., sauf mardi.
Mat. dimanche à 15 heures.

I tried writing here, at the Closerie des Lilas, Hemingway's haunt.

"No peeking, Bev!" Paris was convenient for men in the 50s.

10

Rue Huysmans: I Party & Write

September, 1952

"Surprise!" I hugged Mother, Daddy, and Liz on their Dutch liner, the Rotterdam, which I'd secretly boarded in Holland, instead of meeting them—as planned—in Paris.

"Quite a stunt, Bevs," Daddy said. "I thought you might do something like that." Daddy had taken a sabbatical from his job as principal of Balboa High School in San Francisco. They'd found tenants for our house and planned to stay in Europe nine months, traveling to Italy and Spain later in the winter. Liz would remain in Paris with me.

The four of us took a train to Paris, Mother and Daddy checking into the Madison hotel. With six months of French immersion under my belt I was ready to strike out on my own, so I'd left Madame Dessart's pension and found my first apartment in anticipation of Liz's arrival. Liz and I moved to an apartment that an English friend, Neville, had vacated. His high-paying American job had folded, so he'd changed to a walk-up hotel. The apartment—at 6 rue Huysmans near the Luxembourg Gardens—consisted of one large room with a combination kitchen-bathroom. We thought it was wonderful.

The Alliance Française, where I studied grammar and conversation, was just a short walk away on Boulevard Raspail. And, in the Luxembourg Gardens, we could eat French sandwiches of thin-sliced ham on heavily-buttered baguettes. Butter, some French think, is supposed to make men virile so the sandwich makers wouldn't dare stint on butter—even for women.

The apartment had gold and white striped wallpaper and a carved walnut armoire for our clothes. In early September we bought bundles of kindling to burn in the little brick fireplace, because the central heating wasn't turned on until September 15. The only window was a wide transom above the plate glass door to the courtyard.

After we moved in, we discovered that the kitchen-bathroom combination was so small the person taking a shower could reach out through the shower curtain to turn morning pancakes cooking on the electric burner. And inches away, in the ceramic bidet next to the toilet, we kept wine bottles to be uncorked in the evening. Before boarding the French liner, Ile de France, I had never seen a bidet, although it was a standard fixture for women in European bathrooms. So to run water over wine bottles in a bidet seemed to us true Bohemian living.

We often walked to the beautiful, flower-filled Luxembourg Gardens and watched the men, and sometimes a wife or two, play *boules*. In those days the midday break was a two-hour affair, so the game could last an hour and still allow time for a proper dinner.

Back then, in the post-war 50s, many French families considered a refrigerator a luxury. But expatriates like Liz and me preferred not having one—thus being obliged to take our European string bags out to shop before every meal. We'd buy lettuce and endive for salad, runny Camembert or Brie, and of course a long crusty *baguette* to spread it on, along with pastries from the *pâtisserie* on rue d'Assas: *Napoléons* or *mille-feuilles* (1,000 leaves), nestled in a pink cardboard box tied with thin string.

And parties were easy. We could fit 20 or more into our studio—several sitting on the embroidered bedcover, three sitting in chairs, and the rest on cushions on the floor. Sometimes at our parties, our guests would whisper, "Where is the...?" Not much privacy behind the gold velvet curtain, and you couldn't be sure what would be heard. So a man would go out for a walk to the nearest *pissoir* (stand-up urinal) on Boulevard Raspail. Paris was civilized that way for men in the 50s, but with nothing equivalent for women, they had to go behind our curtain—or go home.

Guests would usually bring wine. Those who worked for an American company or the Embassy sometimes brought gin or bourbon from the PX. We also sometimes had American World War II veterans who—on the G.I. Bill—received $65 a month if enrolled in the Sorbonne or other accredited college. With cheeses, *pâté*, and Edith Piaf singing on a 33 LP, the party could go on and on. Since our apartment faced the courtyard, our closest neighbors were the concierge and his wife, who never seemed to mind the melancholy songs.

Actually, they had personally dealt with Piaf's themes. One rainy day, white-haired Madame Ramonde was sad and talkative, and told me about it. "My mother had a bad liver attack and I went to Montpellier for a week to take care of her. When I came back, there was another woman in our bed. Monsieur said to me, 'You go back to Montpellier.' But I said, 'No. This is my home. She is the one to leave.' And the woman did."

But after that, Madame told me, *la grande amitié* (the great love) was over. So she groomed her white poodles and, I suppose, grieved.

* * *

I'd gotten my main freelance assignments through a contact at the American Church on the quai d'Orsay. Pastor Clayton Williams had introduced me to Phillip Whitcomb, who ran John

MacNair's *European News Service* and assigned me the first of many home fashions stories. In those days, if you were a woman, it was assumed you were an expert on home decor.

The office of my editors, Philip Whitcomb and Waldo Wallis, was located at 56 rue Fauberg St. Honoré. I'd taken a taxi to my first appointment at *MacNen's* (as the news service was nicknamed), not sure where the office was. That ride probably cost more than I was paid for the story. However, they always gave me copies of my articles to put in my string book.

Besides writing about fashion shows at Schiaperelli and Paquin, another MacNen assignment was an interview, in my fairly elementary French, with Colette Gueden, a fabric designer at *Au Printemps* (Springtime) department store. Here I was, in gloves borrowed from Liz—and with a run in my stocking from climbing into another taxi—reporting the trends in French home fashions.

I'd also gotten assignments to write stories from Peter du Berg, the editor of *Unesco Features*, 19 avenue Kléber, to be translated and printed in newspapers all over the world. Those paid a huge $50 per story. My first was a piece on the Alliance Française, about tourists socializing and communicating with each other in beginning French. That story could be run today, since the Alliance Française is still thriving in the same building on Boulevard Raspail. But these days, students are given computer printouts instead of having to copy lists of trees, flowers, fish, and furniture from a chalkboard into their notebooks.

Quite a few of my friends those days were writers. One, a slender woman with long blond hair, was fortunate enough to have the name Virginia Woolf. She was a copywriter for the snobbish J. Walter Thompson advertising branch in Paris where they loved to be able to say to a client: "We've assigned our writer Virginia Woolf to your account."

Sometimes I'd call Virginia for lunch. In their Paris office, with a lot of deposed Eastern European royalty around, someone would frequently answer the phone with, "Just a minute. Madame Woolf is busy. La Princesse Natasha (or perhaps Frederika) will take your message."

Of the various writers in my circle in those days some became famous. Most did not. But you didn't have to worry much if your name was Virginia Woolf.

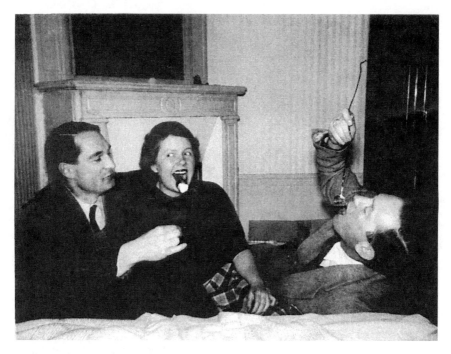

Marshmallows at Bev's apartment with John Walton & Neville Beale (right)

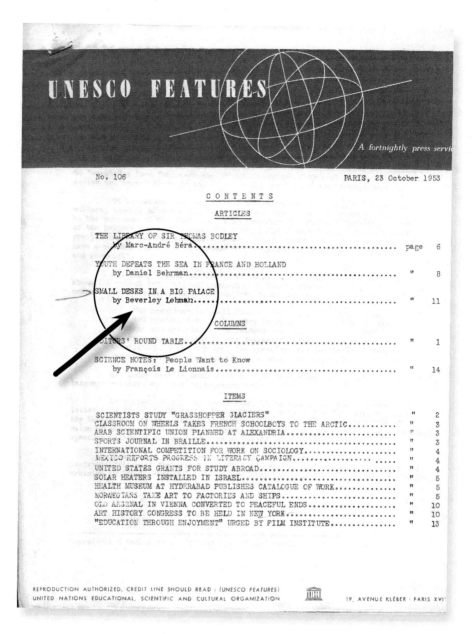

UNESCO FEATURES

A fortnightly press service

No. 106   PARIS, 23 October 1953

C O N T E N T S

ARTICLES

COLUMNS

ITEMS

REPRODUCTION AUTHORIZED, CREDIT LINE SHOULD READ : (UNESCO FEATURES)
UNITED NATIONS EDUCATIONAL, SCIENTIFIC AND CULTURAL ORGANIZATION   19, AVENUE KLÉBER · PARIS XVI

At last—I'm a free-lance writer for UNESCO features

Bev & friend Jim in the *Bois de Boulogne*

11

Egyptians & Student Demonstration

October, 1952

"Don't forget to ask the Egyptians," I said to Liz, as we left the apartment together—she with empty Beaujolais bottles in her string bag. She was going to the wine store, where she'd return the bottles, buy full ones, and continue on to the American Club on Boulevard Raspail.

"I know I'll find some of them at the club—in the pool," she said.

"Of course, Liz. They're very clean." The American Club had not only a swimming pool, but also accompanying showers—something lacking in most Left Bank apartments—so its membership was strong.

We were planning the monthly party at our apartment. We'd invite other expatriates, pour each one a glass of *vin ordinaire*, then let the conversation begin.

We'd invite the Egyptians—Ahmed, Mahmoud, Said, Ayoub and Tarik—and English John and Neville, and Joan, my old roommate from the days at Madame Dessart's pension. And brunette Betty Southard, of course, a sometime law student from American University in D.C., whom I'd become good friends with at the Alliance Française. Betty had brown eyes and olive skin and a merry, infectious laugh. Also a few French people from my editorial office, *MacNen's*, where I'd been able to sell two feature stories. Yes—I was starting to feel like a writer.

At an earlier party, Ahmed, Said and Mahmoud, the center

of the Egyptian crowd, had soon found partners: Ahmed with Betty; dark-eyed, long-lashed Said with petite Therese, who'd traveled with our family to Scandinavia and Italy; and handsome, curly-haired Mahmoud, who usually brought his guitar, sometimes dated me. Tall Ayoub, who loved to dance, was often Liz's date.

Betty had her "first time" with Ahmed. "It's not that great. It hurts," she told me—still a relative innocent who liked kissing and petting. But pretty soon she stopped complaining.

"Every night he thinks up different positions," she told me, "and he has a sexy mouth." I thought his mouth was too big, too full-lipped—not attractive at all—but of course didn't say that. I was to have my own "first time" some six months later with a Canadian graduate student named Ted.

At those parties in our apartment music was Mahmoud's guitar, and, of course, our records. We played either 45s or LPs of diminutive, soulful Edith Piaf, "The Sparrow." Also Charles Trenet and Leo Marjane, as well as American big bands—the Dorseys, Paul Whiteman and Glenn Miller. There really wasn't enough room for dancing in the studio apartment, but one or two couples sometimes managed a two-step.

Among the partygoers was Tarik, a good-looking, redheaded Egyptian. "*Un Juif*," someone in the room had whispered. I knew there was anti-Semitism among some of the French—my concierge's eyes had darkened when he opened the *Figaro* and jabbed a thick finger at a picture of President Pierre Mendès-France—but certainly not, I'd thought, among our cosmopolitan friends. And I didn't sense any at those parties, except that one whisper.

Of course I'd have to tell English John that I'd invited the Egyptians. He had objected after the last party: "How can you expect me to sit next to people who have killed my countrymen?"

I hadn't thought about the Suez War. What had Scarlett O'Hara said? "War, war, war. If you say war just once again, I'll go in the house and slam the door."

But I was pretty sure John would come.

Liz and I had arranged everything at the apartment—wine glasses on trays and nuts and crackers in bowls—ready for the evening party. I was going to buy some daisies and take them home while Liz went to the wine shop for wine, and the American Club for guests.

We walked another block together. Then a hissing sound, "*Assassin, Assassin.* Ridgeway—*Assassin.*"

"Watch out, Bev. A big crowd's coming." We both squeezed out of the way into a café entrance.

A group of about 30 students, marching in formation, shouted, "*Assassin, Assassin.*" (a-sa-SAN). "What do they mean, 'Ridgeway—assassin'?" I asked. "We're on their side."

The students were opposing General Matthew Ridgeway who had commanded the 82nd Airborne in World War II, and later, UN troops during the Korean War. He had now replaced Dwight Eisenhower as the Supreme Allied Commander in Europe for the fledgling NATO.

"There was something in the Paris *Trib*," Liz told me. "I guess Ridgway upset the Europeans by hiring mostly Americans on his staff."

"'Assassin'—this seems a little extreme," I said.

Demonstrations were always interesting. Sometimes they'd be pro-Communist. Sometimes they'd be non-political, simply objecting to the food in student restaurants or the price of tuition. We didn't know enough to be afraid of the marchers. Of course they would like us. We loved Paris and we loved *them*.

Bev with 3 Swiss students

Ted, (right) my first true love, and student in Paris café

12

Meeting Ted, My First True Love

Spring, 1953

I'd always liked swarthy types—dark haired, olive skinned French or Italian—so it still amazes me that my first real love, after a year in Paris, was a fair skinned Canadian from Vancouver, much like the boys next door.

But this was Paris, and my *grand amour*—whether swarthy or blond, tall or short— happened when it happened: two desks down from mine in the French conversation class at the Alliance Française. Ted stood up to give me room to get by—tall—really tall, six foot two maybe. And a big smile with straight, white teeth.

"Merci, Monsieur."

"You're a Californian, I can tell by your accent," he whispered in French, breath just barely ruffling my hair. "Not the hard sound of the New Yorkers." Those days, a compliment on my accent was better than on a dress or hairdo.

"Count yourselves off into groups of five," the slim, dark-haired teacher said, and Ted moved into my group, though that made six. He sat right next to me and I was hardly aware of anything but his presence. Still, I managed to keep up with the conversation. Twenty minutes of talk about food and transportation in our countries, then back to our seats for general discussion, writing new words, and—finally!—dismissal.

As I knew he would, he followed me out to Boulevard Raspail, then, "Let's go to the Luxembourg Gardens."

Sandwiches from the café—bread with ham and plenty of butter —which we ate, stretched out on a private, grassy spot, well away from the green metal chairs where nannies watched their charges. A third of a sandwich, a few kisses, and I knew this was it. A mild, decidedly unswarthy Canadian was to be my first true love.

We had a couple of things in common: we were both North Americans—with Vancouver just a short flight from California—and, importantly, both working hard on our French. Ted, more intellectual than I, was writing a thesis on the French symbolist poet Stéphane Mallarmé for a doctorate at the Sorbonne. Ted lived in the Canadian house at Cité Universitaire, just a subway ride from the Latin Quarter, where a lot of foreign students lived in their own country's houses. I considered living there very unFrench, but of course didn't say so.

It was wonderful having a boyfriend—I thought about him the minute I woke up and could hardly wait to see him throughout the day. Many kisses, and then: "Could we make real love sometime if I'm real careful?" We could and we did. At 26, I became a woman.

Pierre & Prix Goncourt

1953

Pierre walked across the room to my chair and, before I could think or move, ran his warm hand up my shin to my knee. Then he got up, furrowed his brow and stared at me. "Your legs. They are very smooth," he said in French.

"Of course they are. I shave them," I answered him in French. It was 1953. American women shaved their legs—even those who lived in Paris. Pierre scratched his head and walked back to his walnut Louis XIV chair. He took a card and pencil from his pocket and jotted something down. I pulled my skirt down over my knees—though nothing in Paris really surprised me.

"Don't worry," my writer friend, Virginia Shaddy, later said. "He's just curious."

That was the first time I'd met this odd little man with wild black hair and darting eyes that seemed to notice everything. Virginia had brought him, a newly published novelist, with his fiancée, Fern, to the rue Huysmans apartment I shared with Liz, who was out at a movie that evening. First Virginia had treated the couple to dinner at the noisy, student-filled Beaux Arts restaurant. They'd stopped by on their way to a café for coffee and cognac.

Curly-haired Fern was French. I was sure that under her slacks she allowed the dark hair to grow naturally on her slim legs. And, on a warmer day, dark tufts pushed out from her short-sleeved blouse. That seemed natural and sexy to the French.

"Now to more important things than shaved legs," Virginia said to me. "Did you read Colette's essay in the *Figaro*?"

"No, but I heard about it. She's backing Pierre for the *Prix Goncourt, n'est-ce pas*, Pierre?"

Pierre pursed his lips, then let out the air in a deprecating French "pfffft,"—meaning, I knew: "We'll see what happens." He shrugged his shoulders to show us he didn't care at all about the Goncourt award, or that the famous Colette had mentioned his name and his book in her column.

Pierre wrote under the name Gabriel Veraldi. His novel, *A la Memoire d'un Ange* (*In Memory of an Angel*), had recently been published by the prestigious Gallimard Press. I hadn't read it yet, though intended to, with the help of a dictionary. Perhaps Fern was the angel. She sat in a chair next to Pierre by the carved walnut armoire. She watched him, and whenever he spoke, seemed to listen intently.

"We're going to the Deux Magots. Hope you'll come too," Virginia said. She shook out her long black hair.

"Yes, I'd love to," I said. "It'll just take me a minute to get ready."

I stepped behind the velvet curtain into the bathroom-kitchen. The apartment was small but still I felt lucky to be living in the 6th arrondissement, near the best cafés as well as the Luxembourg Gardens and the Alliance Française. I smoothed on my new bronze L'Oréal lipstick, grabbed my black wool coat, and we all stepped out into the courtyard, past red rosebushes the concierge had planted to hide the two garbage cans. We strolled along rue Huysmans and Boulevard Raspail, cutting through to rue de Rennes until we reached St.-Germain-des-Prés and the Deux Magots café. It seemed appropriate to drink at such a famous literary café, one frequented by Jean-Paul Sartre, when someone in our party might be about to win a prestigious prize.

As it turned out, Pierre didn't win that prize. In 1954, however, he was awarded the *Prix Fémina*. Not quite as important. But important enough to make him think he was, to decide with his mother that Fern should have a nose job, and to tell us all how to succeed with our own writing. I remember him in a well-pressed suit, shaking our hands and accepting congratulations. *"Il faut travailler, travailler, travailler."* ("You must work, work, work.") he said, almost clicking his heels.

His smugness was maddening, partly because he was right. None of us expatriates worked very hard. We wrote a few pages now and then, but spent most of our time sitting in cafés where we talked about writing.

The following year Pierre was to put me into a novel, *La Machine Humaine.* I was a sexy, robot-like, young woman living in California—a little too plump, with legs shaved, buffed, and powdered. He even had me serving red wine with ice cubes. He'd used the name "Bev" for the character, with Fischer as the last name, to avoid lawsuits I suppose. But my own name "Lehman" appeared as *"chez* Lehman" (at the Lehman house) in a carelessly-edited sentence. It was a dumb book, easy to read even without a dictionary. Mortified about the chilled red wine and being called overweight, I never told a soul back then about my second life as a major character in a French novel by an award-winning writer. Now, years later, I wish I'd kept my original copy.

Recently I was able to order the white paperback book, 60 years old—its thick but fragile pages folded in the original quartos. Sitting in my study, I slit them with a letter opener to read again of my escapades as a robot-like woman. Of course, I was the first person in all those years to read that copy.

Luxembourg: Dancing in "City Hall"

1953

One weekend the Luxembourgers put up street decorations—baskets of multi-colored flowers and colored streamers on tall, iron street lamps—for the marriage of the grand duchy's son. Then they never took them down. They held so many fêtes, with so little time between, that they'd decided it was pointless.

On another weekend I drove to their tiny country with my writer friend, black-haired Virginia, and my art lover friend, Helen, in Helen's Morris-Minor.

On the way north to Luxembourg, we stopped in Reims, a part of France we hadn't visited, which the pages of our *Guide Michelin* said was famous for its champagne and its Cathedral, Notre Dame de Reims. In a sidewalk café, we snacked on bowls of café au lait, croissants and crusty baguettes with sweet butter and strawberry jam. We studied the champagne list: an 1843 Krug, an 1847 Mumm—both of which we'd tried in America. Another Reims champagne, Henriot, 1808, was unfamiliar, so we all ordered that.

We raised our glasses, sipping that champagne aged in tunnels and caves that formed a sort of maze deep under the city. Carved from chalk, some of those passages dated back to Roman times.

Then we drove along the wide rue de Vesle, the main street, which traversed the entire city of Reims. We passed through

Place Royale with its statue of Louis XV, till we reached the great gothic cathedral which formerly had been a site for the coronation of French kings. There Helen insisted we take the time to park and go in so she could photograph its 13ᵗʰ Century stained glass windows, especially the rose window with its intricate mosaic of colored glass, which graced the main portal.

The great champagne houses in Reims offered tours and tasting, but we didn't want to arrive in Luxembourg too late.

By early evening we reached that little country, which seemed to be built all on a rock. Streets were indeed decorated not only with baskets of flowers but also lighted carousels and hanging metal figures of saints swinging in the breeze. Music was emerging from a stately white stone building in the main square.

I rolled down the rear passenger window of the Morris-Minor and called to a dark-haired young man walking near the car, "*Qu'est-ce que c'est*—(What's that?)"

"*Une fête*—(a fair)," said the young man. "We have one every Saturday night. You can park over there by the church—or anywhere."

We parked, walked over to the white stone building, and pulled open a carved wood door. Inside, a huge room was decorated with swinging bangles and more colored streamers. An orchestra was playing slow jazz and couples of all ages were dancing. As soon as we walked in, a number of young men rushed over and asked us to dance. In fact, it seemed as if half the 400,000 Luxembourgers were there, all wanting to dance with American girls. Since there were only three of us, we were the belles of the ball. All those young men were good-looking, well fed and smiling. They drank rather a lot, but nobody seemed to be drunk while we were there.

"Is this the city hall?" I asked my first partner, a tall, freckled redhead.

"No," he laughed as he swung me around, my pleated paisley skirt billowing out. "This building is just for parties and celebrations. I don't think we have a city hall."

"Really?" I said. I thought he must be pulling my leg. "Who regulates things? Who passes laws?"

"We don't need them. No one ever passes a law in Luxembourg. I suppose you think that's terrible."

"Yes, I certainly do," I said. "But maybe we'll come back again next month."

I later bought a Renault to get around in.

Freddie, the Black Marketeer

Spring, 1953

"Psst. *Ici*—Over here," whispered a man's deep voice with a slight French accent.

"Oh, it's Freddie. *Bonjour*, Freddie!" one of the women in the typing pool called out.

"Shh!" Freddie d'Aries, a slim, full-lipped man in a black suit, hair slicked down with Vaseline, glanced furtively around the office. The building on rue St. Florentin that housed my new workplace had been converted from a 17th Century château. Pink cupids cavorted on the white office walls, and the 12-foot painted ceiling featured religious figures praying, bowing, shaking fists at half-dressed women, and fleeing pursuers in chariots.

Freddie then ran over to my cubicle with its long switchboard and handed me a dozen three by five cards, each with handwritten names or initials. On each card were clipped several colorful franc notes. "Here, I'll pick these up later. They're for people who aren't here today."

"Hey, I can't take those. I'm not a moneylender!" I said. But he'd already dashed along a white and gold corridor to another part of the office, so I quickly stuck the money in my top drawer. I'd just gotten the job a few weeks before and, since I couldn't operate the switchboard very well, was trying to handle other things properly.

Minutes later, Freddie reappeared with more initialed cards and scurried around the large room, handing out francs to appropriate people. I'd ordered my own francs from Freddie the week before, so that particular afternoon he handed me 20,000 francs—in four rustling paper bills clipped to a card—in exchange for $50 in American Express traveler's checks.

"Don't count it now," he said. But I didn't need to. We all knew Freddie. He collected the cards and francs he'd left with me, pocketed them and, after a quick look around, slipped out a side door I'd never noticed before. Our company paid us in dollars and Freddie, a regular weekly visitor to this office, was always prepared to provide 400 francs (the Swiss rate) for an American dollar—much better than the 350 or 355 the local banks would give. Besides, it was fun to have our own black marketeer, and such a dramatic one at that.

My sister wouldn't change her money with him. "I'm not dealing with the black market," Liz would say, so she took her dollars to American Express. However, even our staid parents got the 400-franc rate through a waiter at the Beaux Arts restaurant where they ate inexpensive but gourmet dinners nearly every night when in Paris. I could have taken my American Express travelers checks to Switzerland myself. But that would have been time-consuming, costly, and far less fun.

That office, CMEA (Construction Management Engineers Association), was an American company, handling government contracts dealing with offshore equipment. All you needed to work there was an American passport and a little stateside typing experience. Among those typists were a couple of artists and at least one PhD—women who wanted to stay on in Paris after their money ran out. Several of my friends, including my pal Betty Southard, and also my sister, had jobs there before I did, though I'd applied twice with no luck.

Then one day my luck changed. Liz told me the secretaries and typists were upset—some of them even crying. It seemed their American bosses were angry that their callers couldn't understand the French switchboard operator. Contracts were at stake and the poor typists were getting yelled at. "You worked a switchboard at Wank Advertising last summer, didn't you?" Liz asked.

"Well, yes, an hour a day when the real operator was at lunch. But there were only eight people and eight cords to plug in." I'm not particularly mechanical, so at Wank & Wank in San Francisco, hadn't been very good at it. I'd sometimes poked the bright red tubes into the wrong slots and once heard a man refer to "that stupid girl at the switchboard." Of course I didn't have the remotest idea who the speaker was—to give a cool look to. But Liz pressed me to try for the job. So the next day, in my best suit and shined shoes, I'd marched into CMEA and again asked Miss Hanson, the woman at the desk, about work. "I'm sorry," she said. "There's nothing now."

"All right, thank you," I said. "And, by the way," I half-turned to walk away, "I'm also a bi-lingual switchboard operator."

"Oh, wait….Wait!" Miss Hanson said. "Just fill out this form and you can start tomorrow."

The switchboard turned out to be not eight slots, but a long, terrifying bank of holes and tubes. The heavy, gray-haired French operator, Monique, showed me what to do. She was pleasant to me, so I didn't feel uncomfortable taking over her job. When the phone rang, Monique would say, "Allo, *oui*," and then plug in a tube. I tried it, just saying "Hello," and it worked fine.

Later, Miss Hanson walked into our cubicle and handed Monique a long, buff-colored envelope. "I'll be back in an hour to pick up my things," Monique told me in French. She came back in two hours, wearing new sturdy walking shoes and very sheer stockings, which seemed to me incongruous. She collected her box of papers, books, gloves, and a few cosmetics, then shook my hand and wished me luck. She was probably relieved to be leaving the angry American men. After she left, I began having problems with the switchboard, especially getting calls out. When one of the executives wanted to make an outside call and couldn't, often he'd send his secretary to find out why.

One afternoon Betty Southard, in a brown plaid dress, tan jacket and high heels, appeared in my cubicle. "I'm sorry, Bev. Hurlow insisted I come down."

"An important call?" I closed my novel, but left it in my lap. (Didn't have to hide it from her.) "Well, everything is." She drawled, rolling her brown eyes.

Betty, taking time off from law studies, worked as secretary for a lawyer at CMEA. Frequently he was drunk, and I gathered from the eye-rolling that such was the case that day. Betty always covered for him, writing his briefs, which saved him and also helped prepare her for her future career as a top lawyer in Washington.

"I'm afraid it's broken again," I told her. "Tell Mr. Hurlow it was working fine at lunchtime." Betty and I both knew American employers took long French lunch hours so there hadn't been many, if any, calls then.

"Maybe I can help you fix it." She pushed and pulled various plugs, connecting nobody, until the final light blinked and went out. Then sitting down on the edge of my desk, back to the errant board, she took her little red datebook out of her jacket pocket, and opened it to the ribbon-marked page.

"Have you been to Versailles yet, Bev?"

"March is too chancy with those huge gardens to walk through," I told her. "I don't do anything in March except museums and movies."

"And cafés," she added.

"*Mais certainement.*" We both laughed. Such sophisticated ex-pats.

She slid off the desk and walked toward the elevator, and I went back to my book—a tedious novel I'd chosen because there was English on one page and French line by line on the opposite. If I had to have a boring job, at least I could work on my French!

That switchboard position didn't last long. The bosses decided a "bi-lingual" American wasn't much of an improvement, so they had something called "tie lines" installed instead and gave me a three-month assignment in the typing pool. Being a journalist, I was a fast typist, so that job meant I could stay longer in Paris, write, study French, meet friends in cafés and continue my lucrative dealings with Freddie.

16

Steerage or First Class to Corsica

Spring, 1953

Everything was to go in the book I'd publish some day, so I sometimes did things for that reason alone—like going steerage class on the 100-passenger ferry from Nice to Corsica—ostensibly something I did to save money, but actually did to make a good story. My friends Helen and Virginia, already in Corsica, had written me about the rough terrain and crazy taxi rides along steep cliffs. We all wanted to experience everything, from Paris cafés and Viennese operas to the wilds of *La Corse.*

Going through customs was easy for an American. A black-uniformed official bowed a little and pointed to the end of the counter. I picked up my white Oshkosh makeup case, which held everything I'd need for my week in Corsica—including swimsuit, notebook, extra sandals and paperback novel—took it to the end of the counter and waited for the others. Under my bra, I wore blue American Express traveler's checks, along with my passport and ticket.

The other passengers in steerage—some laborers with suitcases of worn clothes and limp sheets—stood back while officials ran their hands around the inside edges of the suitcases, feeling for drugs, I suppose. But no incidents. Everybody made it aboard. The trip was to be a romantic adventure, with singing in French and Italian. I started to follow the dark-haired passengers, but then was tapped on the shoulder by a tall woman in a pale blue and white suit with shoulder-length brown hair.

"Madame, the captain invites you to have a First Class cabin."

"But, but." This was not my plan at all!

"No charge. Compliments of the captain." She smiled as if promising me a fine gift, rather than ruining my story on the very first page. "My name is Suzanne. I'll show you the cabin," she said. She walked me around a corner and up a short flight of stairs, then opened the door to a large, white room far from the singing and joking in steerage. But—I realize now—safe as the flowered chintz bedroom back in my St. Francis Wood home. On the table sat a round wicker basket of apples, purple grapes and white cheese, covered with cellophane and topped with a red satin bow.

"Please thank the captain," I told Suzanne, "but I really don't want to stay here. I want to be with the others."

"But you must. You're the only American. The captain insists." I had tried to blend in. For instance I'd buried my brown and white saddle shoes deep in a footlocker in Paris. But unsuccessfully, it seemed. Suzanne left, shutting the door with its gleaming brass doorknob behind her.

Through the porthole the sunset burned a passionate red on the water. Singing and laughter drifted up from the steerage deck. Soon they'd be dancing, perhaps making love. I kneeled down, opened my white case, and pulled out—from beneath neatly folded underwear—my novel: a contraband copy of Henry Miller's *Tropic of Capricorn*.

Writing at the Dôme & Seeing Sam Francis

Spring, 1953

Iturned on the reading lamp by my chair and opened my notebook, but immediately switched off the lamp again. I stared out the garret window at the steep rooftops of buildings with their twinkling lights. I was stuck.

"If you can't write here, you can't write anywhere!" my poet friend, Virginia Shaddy, had said the evening I first showed her my new garret at #3 Square Port-Royal.

Liz had returned to San Francisco—and a boyfriend—with our parents, so the apartment on rue Huysmans was a little too expensive. And I'd always wanted to live in a romantic cold water garret. After returning from Corsica, the search was on: and I finally found it.

On the 7th floor, one flight higher than the elevator went, it had a slanted ceiling like the garrets in operas—*La Traviata* and *La Bohème*—and I could look out over half the city. The toilet room and running water tap were in the hall, to be shared with the other tenants. This floor had been inhabited by servants in these *chambres à bonnes*, but now housed artists and would-be writers.

So I had a garret on the Left Bank of Paris, all one should need to write a great novel—or at least the article I'd promised Mr. Willis of *MacNen's*. But it wasn't enough for me. I needed people around: a newsroom or library or, in this city, a café. Yes, that would help.

I picked up my jacket, put my notebook and a pencil in my pocket and walked out of the room. Standing by the elevator door, I heard the dull clash of iron some floors below and cries of *"l'ascenseur, s'il vous plaît!"* ("Elevator, please!") from another tenant. That meant either the elevator was out of order or, as often happened, the outer door had been left open. The latter was more likely the case, as people frequently "held" the elevator at their floor while returning to their apartment for something they'd forgotten. So I decided to take the stairs.

I ran down the six flights and a little dizzily walked out into the square. The night air felt warm as I passed the concierge's cage—by day a telephone booth—where he was snoring peacefully, an open magazine on his lap.

Rue de la Santé was calm and shadowy. I wasn't afraid, for I knew every shadow—the laundry, the glass-fronted *boulangerie* (bakery), and the square apartment building next to it. I walked down the narrow, tree-lined street into the boulevard, which became noisier, livelier, with voices and taxi horns as I approached the Montparnasse-Raspail intersection.

I wandered past familiar stores, the movie theater, and cafés where the students, artists, and theater-goers were each drinking their final coffee, to be followed perhaps by another final coffee. They were all talking, laughing, smoking, and telling the same story over again in a slightly different way, just to put off going home for the night.

I walked to the Dôme and took a round wicker table on the broad, crowded terrace. It was too mild for the waiters to put up the portable glass walls. Couples strolled and stopped to kiss; artists at the tables around me sketched on their pads, and writers scribbled words on paper.

I ordered a coffee, lit a Gitane and opened my notebook to the notes I'd taken on French furniture designs. I was determined to finish my freelance assignment for Mr. Willis. He'd said he wanted to run it in an American trade journal, *Furniture Age*. Although I didn't know much about furniture and interior design, I could always ask questions and get enough information for a story.

It was much easier for me to write with people nearby, so in 45 minutes, after a second coffee, I'd finished my piece. In the morning I'd type it up on my portable Remington, using my bed as a desk with my chair set against it.

Now I looked around the café. There was the painter, Sam Francis—bulky, with slightly unkempt straight hair, whose huge abstract paintings were beginning to sell. Sam was sitting with his girlfriend, Annabelle—slender, with brown hair curled slightly under in a pageboy.

Their sex life was always evident. At the American Club where we often went for showers and a swim, Sam would call into the women's shower room—"Annabelle, it's time to go. Are you wet?" She'd raise her eyebrows and laugh, throatily. "Wet? What do you think? Aren't I always?"

Annabelle was a typist for an American company and, despite Sam's beginning success, undoubtedly made more money than he did. Annabelle wanted to paint as well, but they both needed to eat. Even then Sam had that glint in his eye for fame—nothing could stop him, it seemed.

Now I put my small tan spiral notebook in my jacket pocket and got up to leave, but they waved for me to join them.

"We're looking for a new hotel room," Sam said. "Any ideas?"

"You need better light?" I asked.

"No, that's not the reason. I can't work in the room any more. My paintings are getting too big. Right now I'm sharing an atelier with the Sampsons. But Annabelle and I need a cheaper room. She's going to quit her job soon and start to paint, too. But not right away, *n'est-ce pas*, Annie?"

"OK," I said. "I'll keep my eyes open."

He waved to the *garçon*, *"L'addition, s'il vous plaît."*

"Oui, monsieur: two coffees, two servings of oysters. *Voilà,"* he handed the bill to Sam who paid with a 500-franc note (about $1.25 in the 50s) and left some change for the waiter.

Sam turned to me and said, "Remember, it has to be cheap."

Those paintings by Sam Francis—huge canvasses covered with drips and dabs of color—would someday hang in museums and bank lobbies all over the world.

Café Dôme—a good place to write

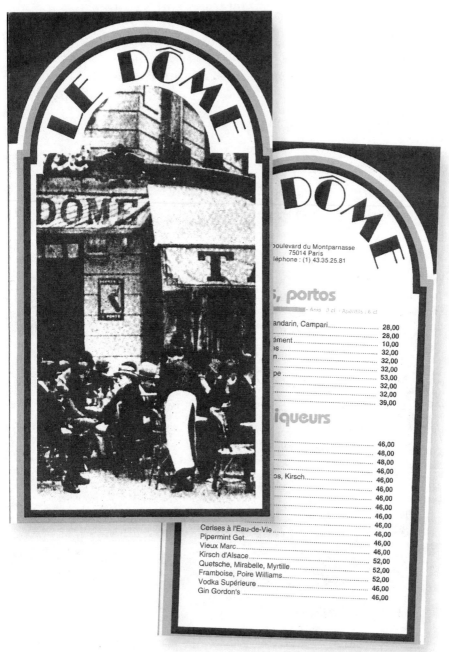

boulevard du Montparnasse
75014 Paris
Téléphone : (1) 43.35.25.81

, portos

— Anis 3 cl · Apéritifs : 6 cl

andarin, Campari	28,00
ément	28,00
es	10,00
n	32,00
	32,00
pe	53,00
	32,00
	32,00
	39,00

iqueurs

	46,00
	48,00
	48,00
	46,00
os, Kirsch	46,00
	46,00
	46,00
	46,00
	46,00
Cerises à l'Eau-de-Vie	46,00
Pipermint Get	46,00
Vieux Marc	46,00
Kirsch d'Alsace	46,00
Quetsche, Mirabelle, Myrtille	52,00
Framboise, Poire Williams	52,00
Vodka Supérieure	46,00
Gin Gordon's	46,00

It was also a good place to eat.

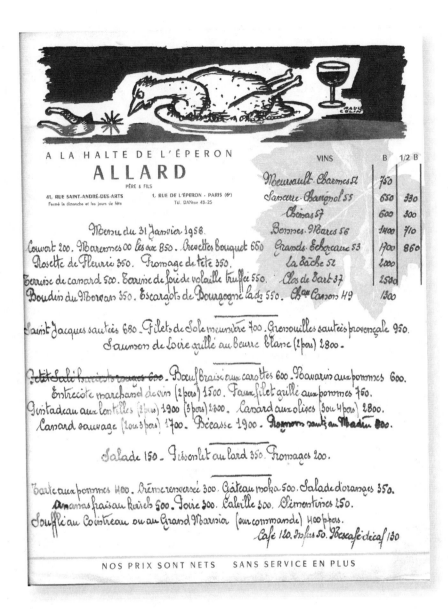

Another good place to eat.

18

Little Gold Watch:
Lost on a Rainy Night

April 16, 1953

"**W**hat luck!" I said. "A table facing St.-Germain-des-Prés."

"Let's take it—before Sartre does," Virginia said. Helen laughed as she pulled out a chair. The waiter came over to take our orders: three coffees and three glasses of Cognac. That would warm us up on a rainy night.

We settled ourselves contentedly in the steamy, Gauloise-smelling Deux Magots café with a view of the great gothic cathedral. I always enjoyed sitting there after a French meal, often a small *tournedos* (steak) and *pommes frites* and sometimes an order of

My favorite little gold watch —
a birthday gift from Ted

cauliflower topped with melted cheese. Crusty bread to mop up the sauce. And a glass of *Cabernet Sauvignon*.

Tonight was special. It was my birthday, April 16, 1953.

Holding up my new gold watch with the bracelet band that snapped open and shut, I suddenly realized I was looking at an empty watchcase. The works had fallen out. This watch was a gift from my boyfriend Ted, and I loved that watch almost as much as I thought I loved him. I had always wanted one that style, and he'd given it to me as an early birthday present. What would I ever tell him?

"I can't believe it. I remember seeing it when we left the restaurant," I said, holding out my wrist. "I'm going to go look for it." I got up and pulled on my black duffel coat.

"You'll never find it," Virginia said. "The works of a tiny watch."

"I might. It's my favorite thing and I'm going to look. I'll retrace our steps from the Beaux-Arts." The streets were getting dark and I wanted to look while there was still some light. Slowly I walked back along rue Bonaparte toward the noisy student-filled Beaux-Arts restaurant, looking carefully along the curb. I wished I had a flashlight.

Some homeless people, a fat bald man and a woman in a heavy grey coat and headscarf, had already found their places for the night. They'd spread out newspapers on grates where the warm air from the metro came up and were lying, huddled together, with more newspapers over them. It was bound to get colder later that night. I was getting used to seeing such people—*clochards* (tramps) the French called them—but the sight of them still made me sad.

I walked past the soot-blackened stone wall of the art school, looking under the square dark cars parked there. It seemed everything was dark, or getting dark.

But not everything! A quick, glistening flash from a car light against a curb a half block from the Beaux Arts restaurant.

There it was.

I picked it up, wiped it off on my sleeve, and snapped it back into the watchcase. I held it up to my ear. Still ticking.

Tomorrow I'd take it to a jeweler and have it examined. Right now I'd run back to the Deux Magots to show my friends. But after a few steps, I slowed down to quiet the clatter of my high heels on the pavement so I wouldn't disturb the sleepers.

19

Gravy Train: Applying for Jobs in the McCarthy Era

Spring, 1954

Now with two years under my belt, I had settled into life in Paris. But I also began to realize the need for a paycheck.

The elevator was out of order, as usual, but I rushed up the seven flights to my Square Port-Royal garret without an extra breath— anxious to tell Helen and Ted my news: The interview had been a success and a place had been reserved for me on the US Government "Gravy Train."

At first I hadn't wanted the job. I'd fought for months against applying for anything so uncreative and completely out of keeping with my Bohemian Left Bank life. And the salary was embarrassingly high. At that point in my career, I thought it romantic to be poor.

But my clothes were getting really worn—I'd been wearing the same dark, subdued wool sweaters and skirts to avoid cleaning bills, and knew they wouldn't last another season. So far I'd had a three-month typing job and had also been free-lancing for *UNESCO*

Features and *MacNen's* news service—which was fun but didn't pay the rent.

Ted, who had an ample scholarship, had kept at me to try for an American government job, comfortably aware that only US citizens could be hired for anything requiring a Top Secret Security Clearance. "The American government is casting pearls at your feet, and you're trampling on them!"

I'd ignored him as long as I could: cutting down on lunches, making it a point to get to the student restaurant in time for a cheap dinner, mending my stockings, and sitting in the uppermost galleries at the theater. Still, the weeks had gone by and my bank account had dwindled. There were summer trips to think of. And that striped blouse in Linda's window on the rue du Faubourg-St.-Honoré....Hadn't I really had just about enough of *la vie de Bohème?*

Finally I'd decided Ted was right, especially realizing that I might otherwise have to leave Paris. So I'd begun my search for those pearls.

The most difficult part of looking for a job was filling out long applications. For the government, especially, there were complicated forms with spaces for clubs you had belonged to in years past, and the names of your aunts, uncles, and grandparents. I'd been to just about every United States and international agency I could think of and they all gave me application forms—but not much hope of a job.

I'd tried the Army, the Navy, the Air Force, NATO, UNESCO and FOA (the Marshall Plan), which a few months earlier had been called MSA and I think before that, ECA. Although I could type in French as well as English, my big failing seemed to be that I couldn't take shorthand. In those days, stenographers were so badly needed that the examiners dictated very slowly and just sort of let you pass. But I'd tried and they still hadn't been slow enough for me.

Helen, who did know some shorthand, had just started a job with the Department of Defense. I hadn't bothered to go there, because the office was small and I felt my only hope was in some giant organization with a typing pool.

One day, however, she sent me a *pneumatique*. Back then, in 1954, you could not leave automatic phone messages, but a *pneumatique*, similar to a telegram, could be written at the post office and delivered to someone's home. On the small blue paper inside the spindle, Helen had written: "Hurry—Defense needs clerks—no shorthand. I've left my black handbag with my *concierge* for you. Will meet you at five at your garret. Good luck!"

I pressed my skirt, brushed my coat, polished my shoes and dashed into the métro, forgetting until I reached for my ticket that I had my own scratched bag under my arm. Still, when I walked up the stairs of the métro into the Place de la Concorde, the sun was shining, unexpected for early Spring, so I knew the personnel clerk would be in a receptive mood.

She was. Not because of the sunshine or my polished shoes. What interested Mrs. Allison, a small blond woman in a green maternity blouse, was that all my relatives were living in the United States and that I hadn't changed my address very often. This would make the FBI's work much simpler, she said—since every relative, former address, school organization, and employer had to be investigated for a Top Secret Security Clearance.

She asked me if I typed well. "Oh, yes."

"And do you file?"

"What? Oh, yes, I do." My heart sank. Filing! Filing was the sort of thing one always puts off until the next day. Did I really need a job that badly? Through the window I could see the black Citröens and taxis moving at the *Place de la Concorde*, and the *Obélisque*, tall and stately in the sunshine. If I didn't file, I'd be taking the boat home. I decided I would *love* to file.

Mrs. Allison said I could start as soon as my clearance was completed—a process that would take "only two or three months" in my case because my background was not very complicated. She gave me about five different types of forms to fill out, several copies of each.

She sat scanning the Paris *Herald-Tribune* and chatting with other office workers as I wrote—struggling with carbon paper that smudged annoyingly on the last copies—searching my memory for family birthdates and names of college organizations. It was the infamous McCarthy era—a friend's father had been fired from the University of California for refusing to sign a loyalty oath—so I hoped that none of the social clubs I'd joined years before were now fronts for subversive organizations.

At 5 o'clock I finished the last page and handed all the copies to Mrs. Allison.

"Please keep in touch and I'll let you know if the investigation is progressing smoothly."

"Is one copy for me?" I asked, hoping I could show something to Ted and Helen.

"Oh, no," she said. "The FBI will need two and of course we must have copies for our own files...."

The iron gate was cold to my touch when I returned to Square Port-Royal. The concierge seemed cross—maybe because the sunshine hadn't lasted more than a few hours. He growled at me that "*les gens*" (people) had picked up the key and gone up to the garret.

"*Les gens*" turned out to be, not just Ted and Helen, but also dark-haired Virginia Shaddy and a young Swiss painter named Georges. I went up, announced my news, got congratulated in French and English, and toasted with the last of the *vin ordinaire* for having become a member of that bourgeois group—the regularly employed.

We sent Georges out for more wine and a long, still-warm *baguette*, and Ted to the *charcuterie* for ham, while Helen and I moved the heavy, marble-topped table into the center of the room, setting places for five.

The garret was loveliest that time of evening, I thought. The yellow candle in the center of the table cast its mysterious light on the slanted ceiling and the oddly shaped corn-colored walls, leaving chipped dishes and cooking utensils forgotten in the shadows. And beneath my window, in those hundreds of houses in the distance, other lights were burning. Living here, of course I was a writer—whether or not I typed and filed for a living.

The next day was Saturday. I slept late and it wasn't until almost 11 that I walked to the Dôme for my coffee and croissants. It was cold and windy. I had my duffel coat buttoned high and my mustard wool scarf twisted around my neck with one end carelessly draped across my shoulders, a fashion I believed looked very French. I saw Helen parking her Morris-Minor and waved to her from the café doorway.

"You know, you're going to have to learn to get up in the mornings," she said. "It's nearly lunchtime." Still, I noticed she ordered breakfast too.

Helen tactfully waited until we finished our large bowls of *café au lait* before plunging the knife: "Do you realize you won't be able to travel this summer? You'll have just started your job and you won't have enough leave." Helen had French cousins she visited in nearby Blois, so traveling didn't mean so much to her. Also, she'd been to Europe before.

I hadn't thought of that. "Surely they'll give us a vacation—just a few weeks."

"No," she insisted. "All the government gives you is a day a month annual leave. You have to work nearly a year before you can take even a two-week vacation!"

I was crushed. Ted and his "gravy train!"

"What's the good of a salary if you can't spend it traveling?" I muttered.

The *garçon* seemed to realize there was a crisis at our table. He hovered about for a while, and finally filled our coffee cups without being asked. Then he left our table to shoo away a thin old man carrying a violin with broken strings. They stood by the door and argued for a while, the musician insisting that the instrument would really play: *"Mais ça marche!"* (But it works!)—and that he should be allowed to enter. Finally he wandered off, shoulders stooping.

Rain beat down on the glass walls of the café terrace. At a table across the room a gray-haired man was scratching his head and staring, pencil poised, into a notebook. At another table a young woman was scribbling quickly, enviably sure of herself.

I knew what I had to do while waiting for the security clearance: write drafts of my stories in a café—the Dôme or a quieter one—and type up the finished ones in my garret. Then later, with my American salary and LWOP (Leave Without Pay) from this new job, I'd have plenty of time and money to travel.

London & an Oxford Graduation

July, 1954

Dear Family,

At last a free moment at the office to write! My trip to England was perfect, starting with a smooth air crossing to London during which I had an equally smooth RAF pilot for a seatmate. He assisted me through customs, carried my bag, bought my wine, and lighted my cigarettes until John appeared, a little too promptly, and the RAF and I parted, forever nameless.

John's getting an MA from Oxford was the main reason for this trip, and I'd been invited to stay with his family. The Waltons live in an old house on Clifton Hill in St. John's Wood, a comfortable old neighborhood. There I reveled in homey English comforts—afternoon tea in a room with rugs on top of rugs, breakfast with kippers, eggs, tomatoes, etc., in covered silver bowls on two carved walnut buffets set along the side of the room. We helped ourselves, then sat at a table where a silver rack of cold (!) toast (cooked at least a half hour earlier) waited for us. Oh, well, when in Rome....

British conversation is wearing. No matter what the topic—the color blue in a painting, or Iago's motive, or the best size suitcase for travel—you have to keep up your end and never let it drop. It's a matter of pride. The French are different: they keep going and don't wait politely for each person to speak. Which gives the foreigner time to rest!

Next day I went to Liberty's and Harrod's which, except for selling Liberty scarves, were not that much bigger and better than stores in Paris or SF. Because of a temporary job scare, though that seems to have been forgotten by now, I didn't buy anything. There was a rumor that the Department of Defense was closing down the Paris office, which would relieve my boredom but not my bank account.

I'd bought John's graduation present—a manicure set in a leather case—in Paris, and French chocolates for Lady Walton. So Harrod's and Liberty's didn't get any of my pounds.

After "shopping," I took a tour boat on the Thames for an hour. This sounds lovelier than it was as it began to rain while I was in the boat—on the open upper deck!

Met John for a drink at a dark, wood-paneled pub, then theater—"Hippo Dancing," written by and starring Robert Morley—very, very good.

Interesting that I once was in love with John—with his Oxford accent—two years of India thrown in to make the accent even more elegant. His reticence in the kissing department seemed strange though I thought it was just "Englishness." Luckily Ted came into my life about then, so John and I became comfortable friends.

On Saturday, the second day, Felicity—John's gentle sister whom you've all met and Lady Walton refers to as "the flower of the family"—with me, John, and two of his classmates, drove to Oxford in a large rented Humber.

The ceremony was in Latin so don't ask me much about that! The candidates were introduced by the dons, and tapped with a Bible, after which they changed from ermine-trimmed black gowns to some with crimson silk trim. Not very elaborate or solemn—not what I had expected.

Felicity and I stayed in a little hotel, the Silver (Golden?) Cross, with leaded windows and dark beams. Our room had a geranium-filled balcony overlooking a courtyard—much different from a catchall French court with garbage cans and neglected plants. The boys stayed at their college, Brasenose. In Oxford, Felicity and I saw another play—Maugham's "The Letter"—quite well acted, but one I'd seen and read previously.

She and I went walking, I chicly in high heels, forgetting the English meaning of a "walk." Strolled through the colleges and stopped for tea or a drink every other hour. Then changed to flats at the first opportunity!

Sunday we all went punting on the river—a civilized sport in which the woman does absolutely nothing but sit back in cushions in a flat-bottomed boat while the man stands pushing a pole into the water. Then the same group drove slowly back to London, stopping in country towns for tea or drinks, and I was taken directly to the airport. A heavenly, three-day trip.

I felt lonely leaving them all—and no RAF pilot to cheer me up. In fact, I sat next to an old woman who silently tatted blue yarn on the plane back to Paris, so guess the vacation ended in typical fashion.

* * *

Movies last night with Ted—"Orphée" by Jean Cocteau, starring Jean Marais. Extremely arty and filled with symbols. A man is in love with death—a woman in black. After he dies, he's choked to "life" because he's a poet and should therefore have eternal life. Very French.

Must close now and start working at my thrilling job.

Love and kisses,
Bevs

Bev visited John for his Oxford graduation in 1954. The friends had a chance to say hello again in San Francisco six years later.

21

Chez la Comtesse de Lansalaut: Learning High Class French & Getting Jaundice

August, 1954

"Yvonne! Yvonne! *La porte*!" yelled the two older daughters of the *Comtesse de Lansalaut* from their chairs three feet from the front door. Yvonne was breathing hard after walking up a flight of stairs from the basement kitchen to open the door and then half-curtsy to me, the newcomer.

It was 1954, just nine years after World War II, and servants were rare in middle-class French families. And here was a real house, with four or five bedrooms, a dining and living room—quite a change from the pensions, garrets and one-room apartments I'd gotten used to in Paris.

Also, the poverty in Paris, with people sleeping on newspapers in the streets near the métro entrances, had begun to depress me while living alone in my garret. So, when I'd discovered—through an ad posted at the Alliance Française—this white house at 72 rue d'Assas on the Left Bank, with its large family, I had decided to make a move.

I'd entered a courtyard and walked past a white-haired, heavily-rouged concierge who guarded her empire—three narrow houses with little gardens. The windows were so low that the youngest daughter, dark-haired Irène, about 13, often sat on the sill, with one foot on the garden path. Nearby were the Luxembourg gardens. My new government job in an office at the Hotel Talleyrand, *Place de la*

Concorde, was a 10-minute bus ride away.

Madame la Comtesse was a widow, raising her son and three daughters on a small income, which she supplemented by having young boarders. When I moved in, I was one of four that included a Swiss man studying to be an architect, a Brazilian girl, and another American girl, enrolled at the Sorbonne, who spoke fluent French. The Brazilian girl, pretty, curly-haired Maria, often wore ruffly pink blouses and was secretly condemned by the fashionable countess and her two older daughters as having no taste in clothes—*"Elle n'a pas de goût."*

The countess gave occasional cocktail parties to which we were all invited, good for practicing my French. "There will be hors-d'oeuvres on the table. If you need anything more, call down to Yvonne to fry you an egg." And she invited us to visit her mother's country château in the summer. I still have the picture postcard of a white stucco building with buttresses and even a moat, which I unfortunately was never able to visit.

A few weeks earlier, I'd gotten the top secret but boring job with the US Department of Defense. As it turned out, the only real qualifications were my green US passport and a fairly uncomplicated background that facilitated getting a security clearance. My gray metal desk sat in a windowless room with 15 safes containing secret cables in manila files.

My supervisor, Henrietta, was a moody young American woman who often complained about the lack of eligible men in Paris and in her home-city, New York. She was homesick, yet she didn't want to leave. Each morning, Henrietta and I date-stamped the yellow cables, usually written in code that we didn't understand, and routed or filed them. After that we typed numerous letters to our friends and family in America, with carbon copies on the Government's vari-colored onionskin paper. We had to lock up the safes before we left for the night, as a uniformed guard would check them. Once, when I'd left a piece of carbon paper in the wastebasket, I got a pink notice warning me to be careful. However, anyone who deciphered my typing on the carbon would have learned no military secrets—only what I would wear to the races at Auteuil the following weekend. At least the job kept me in Paris, near the cafés and near Ted— although I wasn't sure if I was really in love with him or just liked the idea of being in love in Paris.

There were other compensations to the job, too, like PX privileges. I bought a fine Kodak Retina camera, a portable Victrola phonograph with some 78 records, and the new 33 LP or long-playing records, as well as American groceries and tax-free liquor. I don't remember how much we paid, but the liquor was so cheap that if we poured slightly wrong proportions we'd throw the drink out. I had mixed feelings about the PX privileges. This was one of the compromises of being French in my heart—as I'd been since I was nine—yet knowing that of course I was not.

Each afternoon I could hardly wait to get out of the office and climb on a bus that would take me back to my new lodgings on the Left Bank. Even after two years, I still got a thrill standing on the outside platform of the bus where I could watch the monuments and the children and workers going home. Paris is as far north as Nova Scotia, so it doesn't get dark until almost 11 in the summer. Ted and I often whiled away hours on the crowded Dôme terrace, having coffee or wine until almost 10 when the sky would turn a deep blue and finally become dark.

The Hotel Talleyrand office was a little too far from Madame la Comtesse's to go home for lunch, even though that was the main meal of the day. And supper there, which I often missed, having dates with Ted, was usually a light soup, bread and dessert. So in the beautiful summer weather, my friend Helen and I frequently ordered ham sandwiches in baguettes, with pears or apples at an outdoor café in the *Jardin des Tuileries*.

I began to feel tired, which I attributed to the stress of a new job and finding a new place to live. But one morning I looked in the mirror and saw, in the dim light of the beige office bathroom, that I was a bit yellow. Even the whites of my eyes. I rushed to see the Embassy doctor, a pretty, slim American woman who said, "You have hepatitis, probably from eating tainted or unwashed fruit. You have to go right home to bed, or better yet to the hospital."

"Is it contagious?"

Dr. Hasselbrook looked in a big book, "Yes, but only for 10 days or two weeks. You have a mild case."

"What about my job? How long will I be out?" I tried not to sound too eager.

"Maybe a month. Two weeks in bed and then part-time bed rest for another couple of weeks. After that you can probably go back—if you drink plenty of fruit juice. That's your only medication." She stretched to put the book back on the high shelf. Dr. Hasselbrook was enviously lithe. I thought, "She's not wearing a bra." My own was a little constricting, as was the rubber Playtex girdle, obligatory among most American women in the 50s.

I chose the hospital—the American Hospital at Neuilly— rather than even thinking about asking the de Lansalaut family to take care of me. And I decided to enjoy it as part of the Paris experience. "No wine, no sauces and of course plenty of fruit juice," had been the orders of the pretty Embassy doctor who turned out to be something of a role model for me. I'd always been a little overweight and I lost about 10 pounds, intentionally, those two weeks. Even in France, hospital food is tasteless and conducive to dieting.

I became friends with my hospital doctor, a handsome Swede.

"I like to come into your room because I can smoke," he said, adding to my ashtray of Gitanes. Those days, 10 years before the Surgeon General's edict, were pretty carefree. Everyone knew we shouldn't smoke, but almost everyone, especially in Paris, did.

I got cards and phone calls. My supervisor in Defense Central Files was solicitous, though I'd heard my absence meant she couldn't take her home leave. At the end of two weeks, Ted took me back to the countess's house. I looked good, I thought, in a French skirt I was now able to zip. However, the second day that I was back, and still spending most of the afternoon in bed, Madame de Lansalaut came into my room and said,

"Je suis désolée, (I'm very sorry,) but you cannot stay here."

"But why? I love it here. And you said yourself my French was improving."

"It's not that. People will think you got sick from the food I serve. And the concierge will gossip—we must *éviter les histoires"* (avoid gossip). I knew there were always problems with concierges.

"I paid her a thousand francs tip as you suggested," I said.

"Je suis désolée...." she said again, which I knew meant the subject was closed.

I was disappointed—my French wouldn't get better; I would miss the other tenants and the family. I thought of young Irène sitting on the windowsill that first day. Also I wouldn't have a chance to visit the grandmother's château the following summer.

I knew the countess was sad as well, but not too sad to forget putting her bill on my carved walnut dresser that night.

Cold Showers in Paris: My Last Spring

1955

In 1955 spring arrived early—after a long cold winter. It came on a Friday in March, then disappeared again almost immediately. But after living in Paris for three and a half years, I knew enough to grab every minute of it.

At 6 p.m., I closed the Defense Department file cabinet, looked around to be sure I hadn't left top secret notes or a piece of used carbon paper crumpled in a wastebasket, which would get me another pink slip warning, and raced out past yawning, uniformed Marine guards to the Place de la Concorde and my bus to the Left Bank.

That morning I had planned once again to quit my job. Then I'd figured up my budget and decided to stay to the end of my contract in August. Not such a long time after all. Just a few more months, then I'd have my way home paid by Uncle Sam— First Class, with all the trimmings—if I went by boat, which I intended to do. Since I'd originally come over Tourist Class on the Ile de France, I'd fallen in love with steamship traveling.

Now the bus let me off near the Café Dôme, where I met my American co-worker Helen, and my boyfriend, Ted, for an evening stroll, soaking up the beauty of that City of Light. We walked by shops and cafés, a cathedral with flying buttresses, the Seine replete with *bateaux-mouches*, (pleasure boats,) full of tourists. The city lay under a blanket of soft light from lampposts at varied intervals and heights. These evening strolls were usually guided by a general plan of dinner at a restaurant or bistro we knew of or had heard about.

That evening we walked along the recently-flooded river, dodging puddles as we crossed Pont Alexandre III and up the Champs-Elysées. Wasn't it here that Leslie Caron had danced with Gene Kelly? During flood scares, Parisians have long judged the height of the Seine by Le Zouave—a huge statue of a soldier jutting from the Pont de l'Alma. When the water reaches his neck, they worry. Luckily that day it just touched his boots.

I walked with the others, but my mind—a little confused— was on leaving Paris, boarding the new United States liner for its first westbound voyage. I pictured the rolls of narrow serpentine confetti thrown at the Le Havre departure, the tea dancing, and also the docking in New York. Then to Chicago to meet Liz who'd arrive in her Zepherette uniform and usher me onto her train and to San Francisco. Finally I pictured me, in my home city, trying to fit in after "being French."

I knew I had to leave. Three and a half years were enough— more, I felt, would make me a hopeless expatriate—and then I'd find it impossible to leave.

The relationship with Ted wasn't going anywhere. "What about us?" he'd held me close the evening before when I'd first mentioned going back home.

"What about Mallarmé?" I said. "Your eternal *travail*?" I ran my right forefinger over the small chunky gold watch he'd given me for my birthday.

Of course he had to finish his thesis on the French poet before even thinking about marriage. And although I loved him, it wasn't the magic a Paris love should be. That I supposed was the crux of my problem—Caron and Kelly dancing on the bridges and streets amidst cardboard cafés and street lamps.

Kay, a colleague, would take over the apartment on rue

Huysmans, which I'd been able to rent again after leaving the Countess's house. Kay knew about difficulties with French apartments in the summer, when the hot water in the whole building would shut off from July 15th to August 31st which meant taking cold showers—or, of course, going for a swim and shower at the American Club—and heating water on the electric plate before washing one's face. Also, since all French workmen vacated Paris in August, any difficulties with utilities would have to wait till electricians returned from the country. And *citron pressé* (lemonade) tastes terrible without ice.

But those apartment problems seemed minor. I'd be ending the happiest time of my life, and that amazing freedom of being a foreigner—with no traditions to uphold, no white gloves.

I knew I had to return to the US—but maybe not forever. Some part of me would always be French.

Part II

Trying to Fit in Again

1955-1963

Homecoming: They Watched TV, Not Me

Fall, 1955

"Leslie, it's Beverley at the door. Back from Europe." Mrs. O'Malley ushered me into the living room. Leslie whom I'd known since kindergarten waved at me. Her eyes, however, stayed on the round screen of the walnut console television—not on my short French haircut, my pointed toe shoes, my slim wool skirt.

Except for the addition of the TV, the large living room was the same as I remembered it three years earlier when I said goodbye to the O'Malleys. There were the windows overlooking Santa Clara Avenue, just two blocks from the clubhouse and tennis courts, and a faint scent of furniture polish applied by Mrs. O'Malley's "girl." In the 50s, each family in St. Francis Wood had a semi-trained servant in a pastel cotton or nylon uniform. Ours was always "let go" just before summer vacation when we would rent a cabin in the Sierra at Tahoe or Angora Lake for two months. That seemed a little unfair to me, but it was standard practice.

Probably that didn't happen in Judge O'Malley's house where they gave parties throughout the summer. And had more elaborate family dinners than we. I could smell a roast in the kitchen and soon heard a whistle from the pressure cooker, which our mothers all had in those days. Then footsteps. The pressure cooker was rushed to the sink and hissing water run on it.

"We'll talk in a minute," Leslie said, picking up a potato chip from the Delft plate, offering me the plate as well as a paper napkin from a pile on the coffee table, then again turning her attention to Desi and Lucy in "I Love Lucy" on the TV.

I couldn't believe it. Who would want to watch TV when their friend was back from Europe with stories about seeing Colette in a Paris café, and with pictures of a camel with its legs stuck flat out on the Sahara sand, waiting for Bev to get on before bending its legs to get up. And then there was that mysterious ring on her finger—not a diamond but worth talking about.

I was extra polite in those days, so I watched the TV too. Finally she began to talk to me, but her eyes and mind were really on the dark-haired man and big-eyed woman arguing on the screen.

Leslie never did ask me about Europe and I finally stopped bending my head to show off my haircut or opening and closing my Egyptian poison ring.

I finally mounted a camel in Egypt, while my friends watched TV.

San Francisco: Settling In & Out Again

1955-57

"Now I've got a sister again!" Liz kept saying those first weeks after I returned to San Francisco from Paris. It was comforting for me to be back with the family in familiar St. Francis Wood. Also, happily, the US didn't seem entirely plastic and crass, as I'd expected.

It had been about two years since Daddy took a sabbatical and we'd all four been together in Paris. Now he was back at work as principal of Balboa High, while Mother was cooking and taking care of our house—neither of which domestic activities I *ever* wanted to do. And Liz had this new cool stewardess job as a Zepherette—complete with uniform and cap—on the *California Zepher*, a train that went to and from Chicago.

My year with the Department of Defense in Paris had entitled me to 'First Class' travel to the States. I'd chosen the first westbound crossing of the new liner named the *United States*—eating well-served meals, dancing and meeting a few society people who traveled with valets and maids.

Among them was a *Los Angeles Times* columnist. "How do you spell your name?" he'd asked me.

"You certainly don't want me in your column—with all these society people."

"Yes, you're the most important," he said. "Know why?"

"Oh, of course, 'cause I'm the only Californian."

He sent me a copy of his column, referring to me as "attractive, wide-eyed, looking for a job in journalism." I loved the first adjective, but cringed at being called wide-eyed. After landing in New York, I flew to Chicago, then traveled home to San Francisco free—but cramped—in Liz's private stateroom on the train.

Her job included major layovers in Chicago—from where she could travel to eastern cities—and of course long layovers in San Francisco. With her own room she could sneak friends, or a sister, on the train to or from Chicago.

"We sleep head to toe—just bring talcum powder for your feet," she'd warn freeloading friends.

The first month at home I spent in lazy luxury. But then I started job hunting, determined to find something on the *San Francisco Chronicle*. I'd heard that the Sunday Editor was friendly, and I knew his secretary slightly—so decided his office would be the place to start.

"Here's my string book," I handed Stanleigh Arnold a black leatherette binder filled with clippings of stories I'd written in Paris. I hoped I'd sound like a pro by saying "string book"—a term left over from the days when freelance correspondents (stringers) were paid by the inch, measured by a length of string on their printed story.

He didn't react, but read several while I waited, "Your clippings are very good, but I'm sorry, we have no openings," he said.

I'd expected a little negativity, so had a backup plan. "I'm going out of town for a while. Can I come in again when I get back?"

"That would be fine, Miss Lehman."

A week later I went in again. His friendly secretary, Nancy Griffin, said the editor was in a meeting. "It might be some time. Would you like to wait?"

"Of course, if it's OK." I settled myself in a chair near the door. I liked the inky smell wafting in from the composing room and the sound of clacking typewriters.

An hour later Mr. Arnold came in, "I'm sorry you had to wait. There are still no openings."

"Oh, that's all right. I have to go out of town again for a while anyway." After the third "trip," when I walked into the Sunday Editor's office, he laughed a little, but I pretended not to notice. Then I waited three weeks before going back.

The fourth time was the charm: "We have an opening for a writer that I think you could fill," he said. "It's for a new home section, called 'Bonanza.' I'll take you down and introduce you to the editor."

We walked across the floor, past the society section where three women were typing away—rather dressed up in black faille, rose velvet, and tailored navy. The tailored one was older—probably the Society Editor, Mildred Brown Robbins. And the black faille with glasses would be Joan Wolfe, whose byline I knew, typing fast so she could get back to the novel in her lap. I supposed they'd all just been to parties and were writing about them.

A middle-aged petite woman was standing at a desk as we passed. "Miss Lehman, this is Evelyn Hannay, the Fashion Editor."

"Oh, I know. You're 'Ninon,'" I said. "I read you all the time."

She laughed, "I just use that name when I have special features. I don't know who invented it."

"'Bonanza' is along this way," Stan Arnold said. "These are the feature sections that come out only on Sundays—there's 'Datebook' with the movie and theater listings and stories about restaurants. That writer is Marian Zailian, about your age." I saw a pretty, dark-haired woman typing from a chart on her desk.

"Then, over by the windows, is 'The World,' which deals with international events." Several 'World' reporters were laughing, throwing large square gum erasers at each other, but then quickly sat down and pretended to work.

"And over there, to the right, is 'Leisure.' That's Polly Noyes, the Travel Editor." I saw a heavy blond woman reading a slick brochure while talking on the phone. Travel writing, I thought. Getting *paid* for travel writing.

"And here is 'Bonanza.'" He led me to a little circle of three desks and a table and file cabinet where two men were sitting, smoking, and talking.

"Miss Lehman, this is Dick Johnston, the editor, and Bruce Coleman who writes about gardens and home repairs.

"The opening is for a 'Home Fashions' editor. If you take it, you'll write about appliances and decorating," Mr. Arnold said.

My God, I hate refrigerators and stoves! I know nothing about rugs and lamps and furniture! He assumes because I'm a woman, I do. But it *is* the *Chronicle*.

"Great, Mr. Arnold. When do I start?"

With both of us now employed, Liz and I rented an apartment in a section of San Francisco less staid than St. Francis Wood—on Gough, near Green, which meant we'd get coffee or drinks on Union Street, then walk through the Marina to the Bay. It was a garden apartment with a large living room—big enough for dances, which we had every few weeks when Liz was in town from her *Zepher*.

The *Chronicle* turned out to be fun and noisy. I met Herb Caen who wrote a famous column, "Baghdad by the Bay" on celebrities and nightlife in San Francisco. Sitting near me was heavyset Art Critic Alfred Frankenstein who pushed abstract expressionism, in style after World War II, with such painters as Jackson Pollock and Mark Rothko. Al and I often talked, but I never admitted my favorite painting was "The Blue Boy."

Also nearby was Drama Critic Paine Knickerbocker, dashingly handsome, with a cornflower in his lapel and a foulard handkerchief in his breast pocket. Generous with theater and movie tickets, he was popular with reporters. I particularly admired him for going out of his way to give a break to minority companies and unknown black actors throughout the state.

Another of my favorites was sweet, sensitive Bob Bastian, the political cartoonist, who, some years later after a union strike, left the *Chronicle* and then committed suicide. He was a private person and, as far as I can tell, no one knew his reasons. I remember his bringing his paper cup of coffee and a doughnut over to "Bonanza." "I'm ashamed of having another doughnut at my desk," he'd say, "so I'll eat it here and then go back." He wasn't fat, so why he had to do that I don't know.

One day a sexy, throaty, dark-haired woman who was promoting a new lovelorn column came into the office of the executive editor, swaggering Scott Newhall. I had walked in there with a proof for Scott and was standing near his desk when he invented her name: "Let's see, Angela van Buren, Beverley van Buren, No, it's Abigail—Abigail van Buren," he decided. Thus "Dear Abby" was born.

Later the always-innovative Scott Newhall pushed *Tales of the City* by Armistead Maupin, which ran chapter by chapter in the *Chronicle*. All San Francisco guessed, but no one knew for sure until the very last day, how it would end—when the landlady turned out to be a transvestite and gay.

While working on the *Chronicle*, I saw a lot of Stan Arnold's secretary, Nancy Griffin. Through her I became friends with Polly Noyes. "Your stories are good," Polly said. "We've got a special travel section coming up. Will you write something about Paris?"

"Yes! My favorite topic!"

"It's on spec, of course," Polly said. "If it gets in we pay extra."

I spent several evenings and a weekend writing the story. The extra money didn't mean anything—I was a single woman getting a professional salary, much more than I could use. But a byline on a travel story in the *San Francisco Chronicle* meant a lot. Polly and her boss, Charlie Downie, both liked my piece and put it into the special section.

In the meantime I wrote weekly stories about home fashions. I wrote a "Home of the Week," complete with pictures by a staff photographer who would accompany me for the interview. Sometimes the photographer would be short, bespectacled Joe Rosenthal, famous for a photo of American soldiers raising the flag at Iwo Jima. And, as Stan had warned, I wrote about any new appliances—including the amazing microwave, about which I wrote "cooks food in a cool oven in a matter of minutes."

Whenever there was a decorating item needing publicity, I'd be invited to a cocktail party or opening. I'd dress up for these parties and flirt a little with a handsome decorator, who would often leave me flat when another man came by. Fortunately, there were many single men in San Francisco and of course at the *Chronicle*, so Liz and I had plenty of dates in those months.

I had a serious affair with David Howland, a redheaded, talkative, behavioral scientist from M.I.T. who had a year's grant at Stanford. We both loved the theater, music and, I thought, each other. David himself was dramatic, presenting me with unusual jade and amber jewelry at Christmas and giving Mother the longest box of chocolates I'd ever seen. He always thought up interesting things to do, reserving tickets to hit plays and concerts. And whenever the Drama Critic gave me theater tickets, I'd phone David and he'd drive up from Palo Alto on the spur of the moment. We spent at least one night a week together, either in his little rented stucco house or my apartment. He teased me about my home fashions job, though I think really admired me for working on a prestigious paper.

But his career came first, so when the year's grant was up, David ditched me and took off for Boston. "I wish I had more time," he said to his tearful lover.

With David gone, I began pining for Paris and talked to Polly Noyes about it.

"I really want to go back," I told her. "I'd like to try my hand at freelancing. Budget traveling. Maybe I could cross the country by bus and write about it, and then go to Europe…."

"Interesting ideas," she said. Then her phone rang—her boyfriend and a long conversation.

A week later Polly waved me over to her desk, "I can get you a junket to cross the country by Greyhound bus. They'll pay for your hotels along the way."

"Wow, what do I have to do?"

"You write two or three stories about it for the travel section."

"Thanks! That'll be easy."

"Wait. That's not all," Polly said. "Icelandic Airlines is on my neck for a mention. How about flying from New York to Reykjavik, stopping overnight, then going on to Paris?"

"I might be able to do that," I felt a little dizzy and sat on the edge of her desk.

Polly laughed, "It's not that simple. Icelandic is *really* budget travel. They have unpressurized cabins—murder on the ears."

Polly got me my tickets. With her help, I set up a cross-country itinerary, including Atlanta and New Orleans, which I'd always wanted to see.

"You should try to get stories in other Sunday papers," Polly suggested.

"OK, which ones do you think?"

"Go to the library. Look up Ayers' *Directory of Newspapers and Periodicals*. You can get the names of newspapers. Be sure they're outside each other's circulation areas. Then go from there," she said. I sent letters to Sunday newspapers asking if they'd look at my stories.

"I got three answers," I told Polly a few weeks later, "including the *Los Angeles Times*!"

Liz got another roommate for the apartment and Stan Arnold found a new Home Fashions Editor. After farewell parties at both places, Mother, Daddy and Liz drove me with my bag and typewriter to the grimy Greyhound depot. My bus itself was large and clean.

After hugs all around, I climbed the step and turned to wave. Liz had unsnapped her blue leather shoulder bag and pulled out a roll each of red and yellow serpentine streamers. She raised her arms, a roll in each hand.

"Don't you dare throw streamers, Liz! I'll be the laughing stock of the bus."

"OK," she said, and stuffed them back in her bag, "if you promise to write—not just stories, but *us*."

Liz got us all free rides on the California Zepher.

Liz worked as a Zepherette on the California Zepher train.

David Howland gesturing at a friend, Bev smoking at party at home in San Francisco.

Bev, home from Paris in 1955, with Mother

Daddy, me, Mother (at right) with guest at Christmas

GEARY THEATRE

GEARY AND MASON STREETS, SAN FRANCISCO ★ TELEPHONE ORDWAY 3-6440

Beginning Sunday Evening, January 8, 1956

RONALD A. WILFORD ASSOCIATES, INC. and JEAN DE RIGAULT

present

MARCEL MARCEAU

and his partners

PIERRE VERRY and PAUL SANCHEZ

in an evening of

PANTOMIME

Repertory of MARCEL MARCEAU

The program consists of several of the following pantomimes:

PART I

STYLE PANTOMIMES WITH MARCEL MARCEAU

Walking
Walking against the Wind
The Staircase
Youth, Maturity, Old Age, and Death
The Dandy
The Bureaucrat
Tug-of-War
The Public Garden

To go up and down a Hill with a Hand-Cart
At the Clothier's
The Dice-Players
The Thief
The Tight-rope Walker

To the theater in San Francisco but with one foot in Paris

There's Something About PARIS

San Francisco Chronicle Spring Travel Guide
Sunday, February 17, 1957

I passed through Paris on a student tour, turned in my ticket and stayed three years. And I never understood why. But every time I made plans to leave I got a funny feeling—way down in the pit of my stomach.

The attraction was certainly not the weather—for except for those two or three sun-filled days per annum when the songwriters happen to be visiting, Paris is enveloped in the coldest drizzle or most stifling, sticky heat I have ever known. Not the efficiently-managed public utilities or the complacent, uncomplicated natives—for in Paris the very opposites are the case.

Yet I, and many like me, stayed on—converting passage-home

money, insurance annuities and occasional honest labor into cold, hard francs.

We lived relatively well. For, though those walk-up garrets and hotel rooms on the Left Bank were often *sans confort* (which means you wear your winter coat indoors and walk down a hall and up some stairs to brush your teeth) the area is filled with interesting cafés and some of the best restaurants in the world.

Dinner properly began at a café with a glass of French Martini—a dark sweet vermouth flavored with a twist of lemon. It was sipped during a delicious period of repose and contemplation at a round metal table placed well out on the sidewalk. At the peak of winter, the tables and wicker chairs were moved back into the confines of the café behind temporary walls of steamy glass.

Around seven o'clock, having sipped and contemplated, my friends and I would wander off to the restaurant we had finally selected. And, in the Latin Quarter, there were many.

We usually studied the menu posted by the door to be sure we could still have such wondrous hors d'oeuvres as caviar and toast, oysters or escargots for little more than 30 cents. Then the entrée—beef steak prepared in dozens of ways with sauces peculiar to each chef, or veal or pork or chicken or duck—always cooked and seasoned with skill.

As the wine glasses were being refilled, in came a large serving of vegetable, often cauliflower with cheese straight from the oven and slightly crusty. Next the salad, merely leaves of lettuce dressed in oil and vinegar, but somehow a work of art. And then cheese—or pastry—or both.

Another decision. Which café to choose for that strong dark brew of coffee so necessary after a French meal. The Coupole or Dôme at Montparnasse? The Café Royale, the Deux Magots or the Café Flores near the church at St.-Germain-des-Prés? Or possibly, the noisy, student-crowded Dupont on the Boulevard St. Michel? No hurry. While waiting for the garçon to bring a scribbled but usually accurate check, there was plenty of time to decide.

I learned a good deal during those days—about art; and how to hold the shell of a garlicky, buttery snail in a device that looked like an eyelash curler; about history; and how to eat as the French did, left-handed; about music; and how to soak up that last drop of sauce with a tiny morsel of bread.

Yet I never have been able to understand why I stayed so long, or why the very mention of Paris creates that strange longing— deep inside me—sort of near the stomach.

25

Bus Trip Across America

Spring, 1957

"Look, Bev. The Grand Canyon is only a mile down. But it's real down!" said Marguerite Smitz van Oyen, a young cheerful Dutch woman I'd met on the Greyhound the day before. I edged my donkey up to hers as best I could, switching and kicking it a little as I'd been taught, but not enough to encourage it to go over the cliff. From the South Rim we looked down upon whole ranges of mountains rising from the gorge.

"Yes, it's pretty perilous," I said. "What did the guidebook call it?—'a trail by surefooted mule.'" I can still hear the crunch, some 60 years later, of a hoof sliding *almost* off the steep gravel path. But the animals would always recover themselves and Marguerite and I made it to the bottom. (Or else I wouldn't be writing this!)

Many of the visitors that weekend were—like Marguerite—foreigners, and while waiting at the desk for my mule ticket, I heard the liquid sounds of French and Italian, the broad flat accent that is unmistakably Australian as well as the R-less dialect of the American South. Strange, I thought, that tourists come from afar to see the canyon while so many Californians, who have only to cross a state border to do so, don't.

The Bright Angel trail trip, by mule, to Plateau Point, cost $10. The price included a box lunch. You were required to wear long sleeves and a straw hat to protect you from the Arizona sun and to weigh less than 200 pounds.

Just before nine the next morning, I rented a straw hat for 35 cents, weighed in, and walked down to the corral to meet Marguerite as we'd planned. She'd been traveling light, but was able to rent her entire riding outfit—jeans, shirt, and hat—for a small fee at her hotel.

Chocolate, my mule, was big, brown and, from the start, unpleasant. I was hoisted onto her, told to hold the reins in one hand and a leather switch called a quirt in the other. I decided to walk her a bit, partly for practice and partly to show her, before we left the corral, whether mule or rider would be master.

I turned her to the left and she went right. Then I turned her right, switching and kicking her at the same time, but she just made a mule-like noise like a laugh to show she hadn't felt a thing, and turned in the opposite direction.

We were still turning to and fro when the cowboy guide uttered a small, one-syllable sound that meant it was time to go. Then he took out a packet of paper and proceeded to roll a cigarette, as an indication, I suppose, that he was a real cowboy. I watched closely to see if he would put a filter in.

There were seven in our party and the cowboy silently lined

us up. He put Marguerite, dark, young and foreign, immediately behind himself, me behind her, two elderly women next and the men at the very end. We rode out of the corral onto the canyon trail. I looked down again and my stomach turned over inside me. At least there were branches to grab onto if you fell.

We descended a steep cliff called Jacob's Ladder going around hairpin turns every few feet. Chocolate persisted in going to the outer edge of the trail at each turn. It seemed that she was off balance, with more of her weight off the trail than on it. I tried to make up the difference by leaning inward. Chocolate noticed, unfortunately, and we both then knew she was in control.

She delighted in tormenting me. Along the flat part of the trail she would lag behind, then run to catch up at the steep turns. I closed my eyes, clinging to the horn, comforted only by the thought that if I went, Chocolate would go too. I wondered if Marguerite's mule was giving her trouble, but she was ahead and around a bend.

We got to the end of that trail and rode along a wide, almost flat, path. Now I could look about me—at the flowering cacti, at the burro sage, and at Battleship Rock, golden and green, in the distance. The walls of the canyon were sheer rock and sand, broken by clumps of brush and occasional trees.

I asked if I could have some water. The cowboy shook his head. "Not till we get to Indian Gardens, where the mules can get some." Indian Gardens was cool and green. We got off the mules and forced our legs to move to the spigot, where we dowsed our faces and swallowed quantities of water before opening our box lunches. Soon the cowboy motioned us back: the mules were ready to go.

We rode along a pleasantly flat trail to Plateau Point and looked down to the Colorado River, a tiny, muddy stream of water far below us which was, unbelievably, one of the main causes of this 217-mile-long, 4 to 18-mile-wide canyon. At dusk we returned to the corral—seven riders, seven mules. Marguerite and I had just enough time to check out of our respective hotels before boarding the evening bus for Flagstaff.

"We're in luck," Marguerite said in the Greyhound depot. "This is a Scenecruiser. For a bus, it's pure luxury." We climbed to the upper level and picked two seats near the front. From here we'd have a fine view of the countryside, well over the tops of speeding cars and Burma Shave jingles. We tilted our foot and headrests for extra comfort and, later, dozing. Unfortunate, I thought, that all buses weren't Scenecruisers.

After Flagstaff, we would tour Albuquerque and the Carlsbad Caverns together. Then I would go to El Paso and Mexico while Marguerite visited her brother and sister-in-law in New Orleans. I planned a four-day gustatory adventure with the Creole restaurants in New Orleans myself, so she and I would meet there. Beginning in Albuquerque, for our lunches, picnic meals saved us money and were more nutritious than a sandwich purchased at a plastic-laminate counter of a low-priced lunchroom. I don't like spicy food so I was happy to avoid the hot chili, salsa, fry bread, and tortas in the fancy local restaurants.

We found fruit and cheese at a deli and, after walking the winding brick paths of the ancient Indian and Spanish "Old Town," ate on an adobe bench under a tree. Old Town consisted of about 10 blocks of Pueblo-Spanish style architecture with flat-roofed buildings and soft contours of adobe. Long portals or porches lined most buildings with benches that were often built into the back walls of the portals so travelers could sit protected from the merciless New Mexican sun. Founded three centuries ago, Old Town was home to some families whose ancestors were the first in the town.

At Carlsbad Caverns National Park, in the Guadalupe Mountains, Marguerite and I took a cold, wet tour through giant limestone chambers of stalactites, hanging downward from the ceiling like icicles, and stalagmites, which were sturdy as tree trunks, rising from the floor. I still remember my rule for differentiating—stalagmites *might* reach the top. Over the ages, the forces of water had decorated the caves and we saw arrays of silvery and white stalactites that made dramatic limestone formations. The "Big Room," where we spent most of our time, is almost 4,000 feet long and 255 feet high at its highest point. It is the third largest such chamber in North America and the seventh in the world.

Once out of the caverns, we warmed up in the sweet New Mexico air. "Do you have your suit?" asked Marguerite. "Always!" I pointed to my backpack. We found a restroom, changed, and headed by local bus to the Pecos River, one of the major tributaries of the Rio Grande. There we jumped in and swam in that pleasantly cool river along which the earliest settlers were the Pecos Pueblo Indians, who arrived about 800 A.D. In 1583, a European settler named the river the *Rio de las Vacas* or "river of the cows" because of the number of buffalo in the area.

Traveling alone again, I arrived in El Paso, Texas, and taxied to a Hilton. I checked in and climbed into another taxi for the 10-minute drive to Mexico, a side trip which produced the only "international" travel article on my cross-country tour.

Next I went to gracious New Orleans. There I stayed four nights at the Jung Hotel, enjoying Creole and Cajun specialties in several famous restaurants: Crabmeat Ravigote at the 100-year-old Arnaud's in the French Quarter; fried oysters at Broussard's in a lush tropical courtyard with French doors opening to it. I'd long heard of "Brennan's for breakfast," so had to go there—ordering Eggs Nouvelle Orleans, covered in brandy-cream sauce, served in a patio amidst the soft rustle of tall plants, a breeze from palmetto fans and the sweet aroma of magnolia blossoms.

But the really memorable meal was at a private home Marguerite invited me to. The hostess was an elderly French woman who ushered her 12 guests out to her garden, handed us a spray to use on exposed arms, legs and face to avoid mosquitoes, and seated us at a long picnic table. We had chicken sauté, tossed salad, French bread and a sweet Sauterne under the lights of seven-foot iron torches stuck deep in the lawn. Remembering those dramatic torches, I could almost move, body and soul, to New Orleans. One of the guests, a transplant from a western state, said, "This is a wonderful place to live—there's sunshine 11 months of the year."

Promising to visit Marguerite's home in a place called Soeterbeek, near Eindhoven, Holland, I struck out solo again, traveling through Montgomery, AL, and Columbus, GA, arriving at the Hotel Dinkler Plaza in Atlanta. There I decided to take a local bus, a sightseeing tour of my own around this famous city.

First we stopped at a shopping center where a lot of people got off, so the bus was fairly empty when we arrived at a big office building. Many black passengers began getting on the back. Some sat, some stood there in the back, holding onto straps. I was sitting in the middle of the bus, and a white woman next to me got up, moving toward the empty seats in the front. "I hate for people to have to stand," she said.

I was a Californian; I wasn't going to move to a "white" area. I leaned against the window to make extra room for another passenger and nodded in a friendly way at a black middle-aged woman a foot or so behind me. But she continued to stand, holding a large shopping bag. Finally I moved up to a side seat in the front, then watched the middle-aged woman sit down in my seat next to the window, and place her shopping bag on her lap. A bearded black man carrying a blue tin lunch pail walked over and sat down next to her.

Beaches, too, were segregated in the Carolinas. Spending an

afternoon at Myrtle Beach, S.C., I noticed a sewage pipe going from the golden sand of the beach to the ocean—on the "colored only" section some 50 feet away. I got used to drinking from "whites only" fountains, but never stopped feeling uncomfortable doing so as I slowly headed north to New York.

It would be good to take a bus trip through the South again, now that Rosa Parks and others have ended bus segregation and all of us can sit anywhere we want to—as Marguerite and I had when luxuriating on that Scenecruiser in New Mexico.

FOUNDED BY HARRISON GRAY OTIS, DECEMBER 4, 1881   PUBLISHED BY THE TIMES-MIRROR COMPANY

Los Angeles Times

LOS ANGELES 53 · CALIFORNIA
MAdison 5-2345

May 6, 1957

Dear Miss Lehman:

We are willing to look at your articles on travel OUTSIDE the United States, and to pay space rates for any we use. We would delete plugs for specific transportation companies or the like. We are not interested in showing how cheaply one can travel or live abroad.

Unless your pictures are extremely good and illustrate your story in a way no other pictures could, it would be useless to submit pictures. It probably would be useless anyhow.

You should know that thus far we have never bought a travel article. But we like your writing and think you might sell us something. We will have to look at the material first, however, and guarantee nothing.

Sincerely,

James Toland
Sunday Editor

JT:mjy

Miss Beverley Lehman
2614 Gough St., Apt. 5
San Francisco, Calif.

---

* The Los Angeles Times has to date
bought every single travel article
I have sent them.

Free-lancing will work!

12 Part V—SUN., DEC. 8, 1957   Los Angeles Times

Ghosts Haunt Italian Castle

BY BEVERLY LEHMAN

I lived in a castle—a real one, complete with tower and ramparts (and, I think, even ghosts)—when I visited the Gulf of La Spezia in Italy.

My home was the Castello San Giorgio, an imposing stone structure set high on a cliff overlooking the fishing port of Lerici. It was built in the 13th century for the Italian militia and was used later as a prison for Francois Premier and is now the vacation residence of vagabond travelers from all over the world.

Officially it's a student hostel, but as the term "student" in Europe is loosely defined, ages and occupations vary. When a friend and I were there in October, "students" included two preschool children, a poet and a monk.

200 Steps to Climb

It took us several days to get used to castle life — every time we wanted to go up or down, there were 200 steps to climb, dimly lighted passageways to cross and a neglected, somewhat eerie chapel to bypass.

Sometimes the climb seemed too much—especially after a luxurious, enervating day on the beach. On such evenings we'd prepare our own spaghetti in the hostel kitchen and dine, picnic-style, on the wide, flat surface of the castle wall, our legs dangling over the edge.

Our wine was Chianti, poured from a raffia-covered bottle or two, and our view, the ever-changing hues of the Mediterranean dotted with the lights of fishing boats.

From our wall we could look down upon the neat row of palm trees bordering the town of Lerici, the pastel houses of the townspeople and Lerici's main hotel, the Albergo della Palma. There occupants pay $4 a day, American plan, with elevator service thrown in. Castle rates, 35 cents.

The castle also has large bathrooms equipped with stall showers — cold ones, but in sunny Italy we didn't mind. We slept in dormitories on mattresses of foam rubber, comfortable even by our American standards. Blankets and linens were provided, although some hostelers brought sleeping bags.

Ghosts Interviewed

The matron-housekeeper is a tiny, wiry woman named Madeleine de Carlos or "Madi." She dashes through the rooms each day, making beds, shouting orders and creating general trauma. By night, she is up in the tower, performing weird dances, chanting to the moon and conversing (it was said) with the castle's ghosts.

Madi is known, with real affection and respect, as "Queen of the Vagabonds." She has streams of white hair, is ageless (perhaps 60 or 70) and has reigned over hostellers as long as anyone can remember.

Madi and her castle are not the only tourist attractions in Lerici.

An Ideal Spot

The town is an ideal spot for a relaxed vacation—you can swim and sunbathe from April to October, take evening strolls in the soft, pine-scented air or while away hours in the cafes, sampling various types of Italian coffee and drinks. (At the cocktail hour, try Compari-soda. It's a very Italian drink—strong, bitter and loaded with quinine.)

Throughout Italy, dining is an adventure and in Lerici, it's an inexpensive one. Cucina Emiliana's is a charming outdoor restaurant, located a few steps from the castle's bottom step. There, at individual tables beneath a bright, striped awning, complete meals are served from $1 up. Emiliana's specialty is spaghetti with seafood sauce.

Fish Soup a Must

We parted with even fewer lira at the Trattoria Lunigiana and found the food ample and good. There, Zuppa di pesce (fish soup) is a must.

On Saturdays, Lerici's market square is alive with localites buying clothing, kitchen utensils and oddments at tables and outdoor stalls. The best place for extensive shopping, however, is the town of La Spezia, a 20-minute bus ride from Lerici. The shops there had the lowest prices we were to discover anywhere in Italy and the leather goods, sweaters and silk scarves were tempting.

La Spezia is known as the Gulf of the Poets. The major poets who lived there were Byron and Shelley, in 1822. You can visit their white stucco house, Casa Magni, in San Terenzo across the bay from Lerici.

It was in these waters that Shelley set out on his tragic voyage aboard the yacht Arie, was caught in the storm, shipwrecked and drowned.

12 Part V—SUN., DEC. 8, 1957 ★ Los Angeles Times

PICTURESQUE.—Castello San Giorgio is shown at upper right. It overlooks fishing port of Lerici. Promenade along the sea extends from foreground to the rear.

26

My Own Travel Syndicate

Paris, September, 1957

Ouch! My eardrums pounded and ached. The Icelandic Airlines plane with its unpressurized cabin was taking off after its short stop in Reykjavik. Vibrations, like sharp knives, ground deep into my ears. I swallowed four times and vigorously chewed my Wrigley's gum. Nothing really helped except the thought that I'd be back in Paris soon.

It had been two years since I'd left the "City of Light"—two eventful years with a coveted job on the *San Francisco Chronicle* and two love affairs that ended rather sadly. Coming back to Paris was something I knew I had to do—Paris would make everything right—with my profession and maybe with my heart.

Grateful to Polly Noyes for getting me these junkets (Greyhound and Icelandic) I felt that now I could really successfully freelance—write travel stories and syndicate them myself. The thought of becoming an ex-pat didn't seem so bad. And, as for healing my heart, my old boyfriend, Ted, was still there. Hmm....

Once we landed in Paris, I treated myself to a cab to the Hotel de Seine where I'd reserved a room. The hotel was just a short walk along Boulevard St. Michel on the way to the post office. There I'd send off my stories on budget travel that I'd begun in my notebook and planned to finish in Paris.

The concierge, Madame duMonde, gave me a big smile. "Welcome back, Mademoiselle. Your friends Sam Francis and Anabelle Evans have moved in here. Monsieur Francis says our rooms are big enough for him to paint his grand pictures in."

"Fine. Then he won't have to spend money on a studio," I said.

Working space was a problem all painters had, but particularly Sam. He did wall-size canvasses, with abstract, Jackson Pollack-type drips of color. In his previous hotel room, wall space had been so cramped that sometimes he had to put canvasses on the floor to work. When he left them there to dry, he and Anabelle would have to walk around them to get to the closet or bed. The latter was where—Sam was quick to point out, with a long look at Anabelle—they spent most of their time.

I looked forward to seeing them. I knew they'd probably be at the American Club on Boulevard Raspail sometime that evening, having a swim and shower, or sitting in the overstuffed chairs by the stone fireplace, reading and smoking.

However, I knew if I didn't start writing right away I would succumb to my horrible habit of procrastination—especially easy to do in beautiful Paris. I was determined to send off two stories a week.

So before I called anyone, or even went to a café, I would type up the notes I'd made during the plane trip. I set my Royal manual typewriter—same one I'd used during my earlier three and a half years there, and same one my father had used to write his master's thesis at Columbia—on the hotel room bed. Then, perched on a chair, I typed an original and five carbon copies of my story about Reykjavik and the bargain flight—skipping details about the ear-splitting takeoff.

Next I prepared to mail four of those carbon copies on onionskin paper to the four newspapers that had published my cross-country pieces—*Denver Post, Dallas Times-Herald, Los Angeles Times* and, of course, *San Francisco Chronicle*.

After carefully stuffing those thin pages into airmail envelopes, I stuck on each one the French stamps I'd bought at the *tobac* next door: one 30 franc stamp, a picture of a woman in a green evening gown labeled *"Haute Couture"*; another (20 francs), a picture of the illuminated Chambord *château*; another, (40 francs), a vertical pink one of the Rouen Cathedral with low houses in the foreground. For 15 francs, you could buy a picture of the beautiful but severe Mary Anne, whom I was sure no editor could resist, so I used that too. The stamps all said *"République Française."* Off the envelopes would go, to those four newspapers I was pretty sure would take them. The papers were listed in the stout green Ayers *Directory of Newspapers and Periodicals,* which— at Polly Noyes' suggestion—I'd looked up in the *Chronicle* library. Ayers said those papers were all in different circulation areas, so I knew it would work to send them identical copies. (Obviously those were pre-computer days.)

Grabbing my tan jacket, I picked up the envelopes and headed across the cobblestone streets for the post office on the corner of the student-filled Boulevard St. Michel. But I didn't get very far that first afternoon. I was stopped by an endless line of chanting students with placards protesting in French, "We want smaller classes!"

So familiar—at least the protest was mild and non-political. Yet certainly I couldn't go across the line and walk as far as the post office. So even though it would be a little slower, I dropped the envelopes in a green metal mail slot on the corner. Then I stopped at the Gauloise-smelling du Pont café, sat on a wicker chair at a round table and ordered a cup of steaming, dark, acrid coffee—my first real French coffee in two years.

Opening my notebook, I wrote something about the interior of the café and about those students who'd eventually marched off. Then paid for my coffee, left a coin in the saucer in addition to the 15% service charge, walked along Boulevard Montparnasse and then Boulevard Raspail to the American Club.

Passing a post office, I decided to send *pneumatiques* to some friends. So I wrote notes on the provided blue paper—sometimes referred to as *pneus bleus*—gave them to the clerk to put in metal spindles or vacuum tubes and send them off. The spindles would go to another post office closer to the destination, where the messages would be picked up by bicyclists and taken to the hotel or apartment building of the addressee.

I sent *pneus* to Joan Carter, who was planning a trip to Italy with me in the spring; old friends Margot Perrona, Helen Dagron, Virginia Woolf, Virginia Shaddy; and—though hesitantly, not really sure of my heart—to Ted.

"How long will it take, do you think?"

"About two hours, Madame."

I remember that we'd used the same system at the *Chronicle* to send corrections on proofs from the newsroom to the composing room. There we'd place each proof inside the spindle high above our heads and it would speed off to the printer.

On Boulevard Raspail, I passed a balcony similar to the one where in the early 50s I used to see Colette standing, getting inspiration I guess. Ted had sometimes told me, when I procrastinated about writing: "I'll lock you in your room, the way Willy did to Colette, till you finish your chapter!" But he was too mild and so was my fiction.

In the early days of their marriage, while she was writing *Claudine at School*, Willy had refused to let Colette out of her room until she created more titillating scenes—something "extra." So *Claudine at School* had a lesbian headmistress on whom tomboyish Claudine developed an intense crush; later, in *Claudine Married*, Claudine's husband arranged an affair between his wife and another woman for his own voyeuristic pleasures. Willy published these books under his own name, Henri Gautier-Villars, gaining notoriety and of course cash. Later, Colette divorced him—a difficult feat in the early decades of the century.

I might have been a raging success, but couldn't write fiction like that in the 50s. Later, in the 70s, and onward, when writing poetry or travel stories, I conquered my shyness and so could include humor or even veiled sex.

A few hours later, when I got to the American Club, several friends were there, including tall, smiling Ted. "You don't need to come here. Your Cité Universitaire has the best showers in Paris!" I teased him, knowing he'd come to see me.

We all went for a swim in the near-Olympic size pool, took showers and talked and smoked in big chairs in front of the fire. Ted, who was finishing his thesis about the poet Mallarmé, said he'd been sending out letters of application to teach.

"I'm hoping for the French department at UBC in Vancouver—that'd be near your home," he said. So he'd been thinking about us. I realized almost immediately that I felt the same way I had when I'd left Paris in '55. I loved Ted, but was not *in* love with him.

Joan Carter came in later, detained at her job at Treasure Tours. "Still going to Italy with me?"

"Of course. It's my second favorite country in Europe," I said. We were going to Capri and Sorrento as well as Florence, and I planned to do stories about our trip.

Ted reached over and lit my Gitane, "There's a reading at Village Voice at 7:00," he said. "Henry Miller."

"Wow!" Almost everyone perked up. Most of us decided to go hear this famous banned American writer. Joan begged out as she had to get up early for her job, catering to sometimes-difficult tourists.

We took the *métro* to the rue Princesse, where the blue storefront with white letters proclaimed Village Voice. "There's your compatriot, Marie Doisneau," I told Ted as we sidled in next to her. Marie was a French Canadian, a free-lance writer on her way to becoming famous. A role model to me, she was absolutely focused on writing—nothing would stop her. Years later, in the 90s, I was to hear her read her own poignant, sometimes sardonic New Yorker essays and reviews, at this very bookstore.

"Glad you're still wearing that smart blue suit," I told this small woman with dark curly hair.

"Yes, it's one of the things I haven't sold yet. Even pawned my typewriter for a few months last year."

She looked a little thin. "Your stories are wonderful. Jackson is sure slow at selling them," I said. I knew she went to the American Express every day, expecting a check from her literary agent.

Slight, balding Henry Miller read from his *Tropic of Cancer* and *Tropic of Capricorn*—banned in the USA—to laughter and lots of applause. I liked his writing—the natural, authentic dialogue and of course the sex in every other paragraph.

Then by *métro* back to Montparnasse, stopping at the Bar à Huîtres across the rue Delambre from the Café Dôme. Most of us hadn't eaten, so the swimming and Henry's porn reading had whetted our appetites for a large plate of oysters. I craned my neck for a glimpse of my favorite statue, Rodin's Balzac, on the other side of the boulevard.

Paris life was much as it had been three or four years earlier.

* * *

Spring came and Joan left a phone message at the hotel: "It's April. Don't forget Italy." We packed swimsuits—"bathing costumes" to British Joan—shorts, slacks, sandals, but left plenty of empty space. A tacit understanding that we'd shop along the way.

Took a train to Florence, a favorite of mine next to Paris,

and after a few days of shopping and museums, journeyed to romantic Capri and Sorrento for lazy swimming, lounging on the beach—in those pre-melanoma days—and more shopping. Bought simple sweaters of fine wool, better than you'd find anywhere else. I wrote "Traveling in Italy: Take an empty suitcase and fill it along the way," which got printed in several newspapers back home.

In Sorrento I had platform pumps made to order—tan calf, which they measured me for in the shop. Three days later when I went to pick them up, the clerk fitted them on me—beautiful, until I stood up and felt my toe thrusting against the front. Solution: had the leather toes cut out. Even more fashionable.

Walking back to meet Joan, I was a little perspiry, with untidy hair, five pounds over weight and had a run in my stocking. Yet a swarthy bicyclist across the road stared at me, stopped his bike, got off, stood there, and continued his gaze: "Bella, bella, bella." To this day, whenever I need a tweak or a little jolt, I think of that moment.

Joan had to go back to Paris and her job, but I had a few traveler's checks left and decided to go to Rome on my own. I hadn't been there since traveling to Italy with Liz and my parents four years earlier. I'd have to cut expenses, but knew I could in Italy. I could live well there cheaply—if I stayed away from the stores.

I knew where to go first: Liz and I had stayed at a converted palace—Palazzo Salviati. In the Piazza della Rovere near the Vatican, it was well known to students and low-budget travelers, with dormitories as well as individual rooms, a reasonable restaurant and a pleasant little bar. My dormitory bed was to run me less than 625 lira or a dollar a day.

Built around an open, palm-treed courtyard, the palazzo's high stone walls were a dull, yellowish color that looked golden in the sunlight. Small tables were set in the back of the courtyard to form a café terrace, half-hidden by trees. Often at dusk came the strains of a washerwoman's song from the adjoining garden where we saw her hanging the clothes she pulled out of her wooden bucket.

Most of the summer tourists had gone, leaving just a few stragglers at the palazzo. They, like me, wanted to see a little more of Italy before going home. And they, like me, were down to their last traveler's checks.

Early that first evening, I deposited my suitcases of Italian finery at the hostel and walked out into the café for my favorite Italian apéritif—a bittersweet Campari-soda—before dinner. At one of the tables sat a couple my age. The girl was busy with maps, pen, and notebook, evidently outlining her next day's tour. The young man was changing the film in a camera.

They waved to me to join them. She—tall and very, very blond—turned out to be Danish, from Copenhagen. The thin, muscular man was Viennese. Our conversation, in English, began with the usual, polite tourist inquiries: "How long are you staying? Where are you headed?" Then it got down to the essential: "How much money do you live on per day?"

The young man said he stretched out his lira by hitchhiking. The girl said she preferred the independence of going by bike. I hastily changed the subject, mumbling about always getting a stiff neck from looking at Michelangelo ceilings, for I—shamefully, unimaginatively, expensively—had been traveling by train.

Then came the exchange of travel tips, and here I thought I could hold my own. I announced that one could get reduced-rate museum passes from the Italian Ministry of National Education. But they'd already heard of that. Also I knew of a cheap guidebook, a 24-hour laundry, and a shortcut to the Sistine Chapel. So did they.

At lunchtime I'd discovered a trattoria where one could dine admirably for 400 lira so mentioned that. Eyebrows went up. Quickly I added that had been my only hot meal in two days.

The girl said she'd stumbled onto a restaurant where you could get spaghetti for 80 lira. It was called Cucina Economica, just around the corner from the hostel. "It's the kind of place where you take your dishes out to the kitchen yourself—the kind where the *real* Italians eat."

But the hitchhiker bettered that. He lived on bread, cheese and wine—had not been inside a restaurant for three weeks. I was losing ground fast....

"Is there hot water here at the Palazzo?" asked the blonde cyclist.

"No," said the hitchhiker, "but you can have a hot shower in the building in back for 200 lira."

"200 lira!" she cried. "Why, at the tourist center in Venice I had a hot bath for 100."

It was my turn—and my trump.

"I haven't investigated the local bathhouses," I drawled as I drained the last drop from my dark red drink. "I simply don't wash when traveling."

* * *

Back in Paris, I went to the American Express to get mail and checks: several from the newspapers at $15 or $20 each. Not really enough to spit on as Henry Miller might say. But bylines were important. Still, I missed not only a regular paycheck but the companionship of other reporters. I thought seriously about it: where did I belong? After a few months, finally, tearfully, I boarded Icelandic again—back to the States.

Soon it was time for my next adventure: New York.

New York, N.Y.

December 8, 1962

"Today is the day I start job hunting—for a great newspaper job," I announced at breakfast to my two roommates in our apartment on East 62nd Street.

I'd allowed myself a month, after leaving San Francisco, to find an apartment, go to theaters and museums, and look up friends.

"A job'll cut into your social schedule," said slender, dark-haired Isabel.

"No matinees, no art galleries," said blond, German Angelica as she buttered a half slice of toast. She'd been living there a year and spent lots of time at the Metropolitan Museum and MoMA.

"No remarks," I said.

Neither of them suggested I might have any trouble finding a job. I was sure I wouldn't. My résumé, all typed up, showed my writing experience on the *San Francisco Chronicle*, travel articles across the country and in Europe. And, after all, there were seven daily newspapers in New York. I aimed for the *New York Times*—every reporter's dream—but could compromise, I supposed.

"Where are you going first?" asked Isabel.

"I don't know. I'll pick up the *Times* and look in the classifieds." I grabbed my slim, black, New-York-looking coat from a hook near the front door.

"Wait," Isabel said. "I'll walk down with you."

"Down" meant a four-flight hike from our spacious, but low-rent apartment to fashionable East 62nd Street near Park. We crossed the street and walked to the nearest newspaper stand. But it was almost empty.

"A *Times*, please." I'd tried to sound like a savvy New Yorker, but then forgot and added the sweet "please."

"No *Times*, no *Trib,* no nothing," the vender said.

"Let's try the stand on Madison," said Isabel.

No luck. As the first vender had said, "No nothing." It turned out that the International Typographical Union (I.T.U.)—a confederation better known by its historic nickname, "Big Six"—had gone on strike. Hundreds of printers had walked away from their clattering Linotype machines and rumbling presses. All the major newspapers had stopped printing and 17,000 newspaper employees were out of work.

The strike was a battle over technology. In the 1950s and 1960s, computerized typesetting systems that would revolutionize the newspaper composing room had emerged. Labor leaders, who saw that automation would cost jobs, refused to settle for 114 days—until March the following year. Seven papers were shut down, four of them permanently. New York as a newspaper town would never be the same.

So I wouldn't be working for a paper after all, and—even worse—all of New York's journalists would be competing for the same writing jobs I would apply for. "Related fields"—they called those jobs in public relations, advertising and magazines. I didn't really want to work in a related field. I was ready for the *New York Times*. And now I couldn't even buy a *Times* to get the classifieds.

As it turned out, I did get some fairly interesting jobs, though nothing like my dreams, and all seemed somewhat phony to a schoolteacher's daughter. I worked in public relations—wrote stories about Puerto Rico without ever having been there; wrote advertising copy about W. & J. Sloane's elegant antiques and carpets; even wangled a job as Services Editor at *Modern Romances* magazine—where the love stories were free-lanced.

That *Modern Romances* job—part of Dell Publications' Modern Group, which included *Modern Screen*—was a little crazy. I was invited to all sorts of luncheons and cocktail parties put on by public relations people who wanted a paragraph about their product—Revlon, Maybelline eye makeup, Singer sewing machines, even Wedgwood and Corning.

"That's a great job—there's lots of graft," an editor friend had told me. But I did have to share the "graft" with my boss and the story editor. We all went home with our share of fancy cheeses—and teak cheese boards, lipsticks, perfume, spools of thread and bottles of the latest household cleansers. Occasional problems arose—once a huge carton of catsup bottles was delivered to my apartment, instead of the office, not too easy to get rid of. And "Aunt Bev's Sewing Basket," my column of tips, made my friends laugh—they knew I used safety pins for missing buttons when I was sure "it won't show."

New York was not all work, of course. There were museums and galleries, theaters, restaurants, trips to Fire Island and skiing at a friend's house in Killington, Vermont. Several friends paid off their mortgages on summer and winter houses by charging a small rent. I often had weekends in East Hampton—swimming, partying and helping a friend with her house payments.

New York was fascinating to me because there were so many different ethnic groups. I heard many languages and accents on the street, in restaurants and even in my jobs.

Our apartment was wood-paneled, full of light and just a walk or bus ride to my midtown job. Isabel had a darling two-year-old daughter who lived with us. I thought, when I first moved in and saw little curly-haired Caroline, "This might make me more maternal." The years were creeping up.

I dated a bit, but had to be careful, since the married men thought nothing of asking young women out. "Why not?" they'd ask, even when wearing a gold band.

But luck came my way, even in hard-hearted New York. I met a writer—Dick West—tall, dark-haired, divorced. He'd tried to pick up my friend, Roberta Hellman, at the Kettle of Fish on Waverly Place in the Village, using his "starving writer" charm she told me. She'd said to him: "I'm engaged, but I have a friend who's an editor. Maybe she could help you with your book."

He phoned the next day and we met for a drink—one of many. And I listened, watching his thin lips and brown, long-lashed eyes while he told me about his boring job with the New York Housing Authority and his great—still unpublished—novel.

In his wallet he carried a picture of his smiling six-year-old son. I showed him a snapshot of my sister's baby daughter, Christine.

"What beautiful children we'd have!" he said.

And we did.

In The Elevator
New York, 1965

Oh, they're already in!
guffawing
testosterone

six writers going down
from *Mad Magazine*
office on 8.

I guess
they eat lunch
same as everyone else.

Dark suits and ties
like other Madison Avenue men
but faces never still

they push at each other
fall against the gray walls
roar at some in-joke I hardly hear.

One looks like the cover picture
Alfred E. Neuman
gap-toothed smile and askewed eyes.

He could be faking the teeth
but certainly not
the misaligned eyes.

I lean small into the wall
out of the way of falling bodies,
thrown pencils and notebooks.

I want to protect myself
yet hear enough to tell
Emily and Lillian at lunch.

No one can beat a story
of six *Mad* men
in the same elevator as you.

I'm too shy to talk
but wonder where they eat
WHAT they eat.

I could say,
"I work for
Modern Romances."

They'd be all over me,
"What do you do there, baby?"
"I'm Services Editor."

Actually, I write about
the dullest of subjects—
sewing machines, measles shots.

But my job title alone
would get me
3 pages in *Mad*.

In fact, I would probably
never
get out of the elevator.

28

Mr. & Mrs. West: Grounded for Awhile

1963, and Onward

"The test is positive!" I told my boyfriend, Dick. He took my hands and we danced around our New York studio apartment. No flowing skirt—just jeans.

I'd known he was the one from our first date. We were both writers and he was lively and fun. We didn't use birth control, deciding to let what happened happen.

"A boy," he said.

"No, a girl," I insisted.

"Twins!" We both laughed and danced some more, to the refrigerator, the bed, the typing table and back.

"I think I want to be near my mother," I said hesitantly—me, a sophisticated world traveler, 35 years old.

"San Francisco it is," Dick picked me up and hugged me, but loosely around my important waist, I noticed. "We'll get married and go right away," he said. "No more days at the New York Housing Authority."

It would be a seven-month baby, which wouldn't do in the 50s. "Maybe we should wait a couple of months before we tell my mother." He agreed.

I told Mother about our "elopement" and then, two months later, phoned her again: "Oh, Bevs, how grand," she said, "and Liz having another one too…. If only Ralph were here." Daddy had died almost a year earlier, unfortunately before my marriage—before I even knew Dick was important.

Liz was excited, "I'll finally *really* have a sister again! And a brother-in-law and niece." We Lehman sisters were united in gender planning.

Dick and I stayed with Mother those first weeks, although St. Francis Wood, with its velvet draperies and tidy rolling lawns, didn't suit our hippie ways—sleeping late, wearing jeans and sandals, and (for Dick) avoiding serious employment in order to write. We soon located a tiny apartment on Russian Hill and, later, when a friend bought a house, moved into her long flat in Cow Hollow near the Bay.

I'd waited so long to have babies that I delighted in every minute of it—buying my first black, sleeveless, maternity dress, practicing Lamaze breathing with Dick, waiting for kicks and turns, and finally pushing out a beautiful, "premature" boy. (Years later Peter joked about his being shoehorned into the incubator.) Twenty months after Peter, I pushed out another boy.

Mother seemed to accept the premature birth. However, I noticed a couple of my side-view wedding snapshots didn't appear in the family photo album.

Things were almost rosy at first, though I had to pressure Dick to not be a full-time writer.

"Henry Miller didn't have to get a job. June believed in him," he said.

"I believe in you, just like June. But it's been four months. Peter can't live on breast milk forever!"

"What about my book?"

"A lot of people write at night."

"I can't. There's not enough time. But I'll look."

Within weeks, Dick found a non-taxing job at the U.S. Board of Examiners, giving tests to job applicants. Perhaps he could write on the side, I thought. Nursing a baby was cozy and warm. Life went on normally. Also I still smoked my two packs of Winstons a day, just as I'd done during pregnancy on doctor's orders—"so you won't gain weight." Yes, it's true! He'd said that—a highly respected obstetrician Liz and I both went to.

Those were blissful years. Having two little boys 20 months apart was easy. One jammed in a Jerry pack and the other holding my hand or Dick's, we'd walk to the de Young Museum or the Palace of Fine Arts, or perhaps take a long stroll to the Marina Green to throw a spongy white ball back and forth.

Everywhere I went, I had a child with me. I remember once sitting on a cable car and turning around and talking to Peter in his pack. He was laughing and saying the brilliant sayings of one's firstborn. Suddenly, a tall woman in a beaver coat seated nearby leaned over and said, "I had a little boy like that once—but he didn't come back from Korea." The woman stood up, eyes filled, and stepped down at the next stop, walking blindly on down Powell.

Peter and Mark grew up with cousins—Liz's second daughter Ann was born a few weeks after Peter, so we spent Christmases and Easters and many weekends in Liz and her architect husband Paul's long narrow garden, or at Mother's.

Newspaper work didn't seem to mix with young children, so I decided to become a teacher. I'd strap the little boys in our VW Beetle and drop them at my mother's to play or nap, then drive to nearby San Francisco State, take a class or two, then drive back to retrieve the boys. Once, when I had little Mark in the backpack at registration, a cheerful student ushered us down the long line to the front, so registration took me minutes instead of an hour. After that, I confess I often took Mark along.

With Mark's help I got a Master's in English as a Second Language, then began teaching part-time at Pacific Heights Adult School. A few years later those schools were elevated to Community Colleges, now some to simply "Colleges." Most of my students were Chinese or Mexican, with some Vietnamese and a few Polish or French. After some weeks of terror—I'd never even made a real speech—I got used to being in front of a classroom. Fortunately we had a book, *English 900*, to follow.

Mistakes always brought laughter for the students and me:

"What did you do last night?" "I washed the TV."

"Teacher, this is crazy country. They give me $20 ticket, but the sign say, 'Fine for Parking.'"

"I want a white color job."

"I like fright chicken."

"We didn't like living in dictatorshipment." This was Anna, from Poland, who looked up, wide-eyed, and giggled when she realized what she'd said.

Sometimes the misunderstandings were serious, especially with the reticent Vietnamese. One such incident occurred when I was leaving the classroom:

"Teacher, excuse me. I have question must ask you. So embarrassment." The Vietnamese woman spoke softly and looked down at the textbooks in her hand. She had been waiting for me in the wide hallway outside the classroom. Three young Arabs, sharing a cigarette in a non-smoking building, moved closer to us.

"Of course, Uyen. Come in to the faculty room. Or we can use Betty's office."

"Office better." Her slender body trembled a little and I wondered if she were about to cry. We began to walk, and then she tapped my arm.

"Teacher...What means 'shack up'?"

The whole corridor became silent. The three Arabs stopped feigning non-interest and put back their heads and laughed. Two women, a Korean and her French classmate, who had been practicing lists of irregular verbs, giggled.

Uyen paled.

"Come along." I almost pulled her to the office, little more than a glass partition, and closed the door. At least we wouldn't be heard. Such a lovely young woman, I thought, wondering what I should say. I knew she hadn't been in this country more than a couple of months.

"Where did you hear that?" I asked gently. "Who said it?"

She avoided eye contact, "A man."

"Here in school? Another student?"

"No. Outside. American man. Old American man."

I decided to plunge in and tell her. After her escape from Vietnam, probably fighting off Thai pirates on her small boat, she knew the facts of life too well—but not American terminology. So I explained in my schoolteacher tone of voice, "Shack up means sexual union—a man and a woman living together without being married."

She stared blankly for a moment, and then:

"Oh, teacher. I'm glad you tell me. How terrible. Terrible if not know."

"Will it be all right now?" I wondered who this would-be seducer was. Her landlord? Certainly not her sponsor.

"Oh. Yes, now I understand. You see, I ask the doctor about bad stomachache. He tell me come in for a shack up."

* * *

Now back in the San Francisco public school system, which governed Pacific Heights Adult School, I was still "Mr. Lehman's daughter," just as I'd been in grammar school. Daddy, a high school principal, who'd had problems with the night school faculty, waved his arms furiously when they'd move the piano and not put it back. My new dean at Pacific Heights, Mr. Alvero, was happy to remind me of that: "It's poetic justice, having Ralph Lehman's daughter teaching adult school."

The K-12 schools were in the early stages of busing, which meant some students had to go to a school on the other side of town. As a liberal, I felt it was a good idea, but I didn't want to be part of it. I didn't want my kids traveling an hour and a half from our stable neighborhood to the Mission District where I'd read about shootings and muggings every few days.

However, the busing rules for kindergarten and first grade were lax. We enrolled Peter in the neighborhood school, Yerba Buena, for part of a year and he was able to walk to it.

Peter's class was a disaster, though it seemed fine at first. I met his lively teacher, Miss Tarantino, in a bright classroom with colorful charts, pictures on the walls and giant cardboard mobiles hanging in the corners. The children were working on art projects, with colored paper, crayons and marking pens on their desks, when a boy in the corner started shouting and pushing at another child, and Miss Tarantino had to walk him to the cloakroom. She told me the boy was slightly retarded, that she couldn't get him into a special class, so she spent 80% of her time quieting and scolding him.

Peter came home with tales of having to give up his milk money or get beaten up, of children's bikes being stolen right from under them, and of a resentful student mashing everyone's clay pots— even the ghoulish head that Peter had been working on all week.

Mark was in part-time nursery school. He was bright and emotionally ready for Kindergarten, but the public schools refused him because he'd been born in December. He knew he didn't belong in nursery school, couldn't beat the system but *could* drop a piece of cake, frosting side down, on the floor, and tie his shoe laces together so he had to be lifted out of the classroom.

We applied for scholarships for our sons at Cathedral School for Boys, on Nob Hill. Soon a call came from Cathedral that there were two openings, Kindergarten and First Grade, which we snapped up—so now our boys had small classes and no student problems that couldn't be easily solved. With their light blue shirts and gold and red ties, Peter and Mark became the first in our families to attend private school.

Months and years went by. I made a new career as an ESL teacher, and Dick continued juggling writing and day jobs. Mother died at 79 after a happy, fulfilled life. (Once my children were born, her possessiveness toward me seemed to lessen and she and I had become very close, which still leaves me with a good feeling.) After spending a long summer going through possessions and reminiscing, Liz and I sold our family home. Several years later Mother's sister, my Aunt Ted in Seattle, died, and left me the option to buy her waterfront cottage on Bainbridge Island along with some money to help pay for it.

I flew up to Washington in the spring with the other heirs— Liz and our Cousin Bill. It was an unusual weekend, not raining and brilliantly sunny. The little house was on Port Madison Bay's Hidden Cove, on low bank waterfront with a 12' by 12' dock, nestled among the tallest cedar and fir trees I'd ever seen. The land had belonged to our grandfather. He'd used it for moorage when he sailed over from his home in Seattle. It was our heritage—one of us should buy it, we all agreed. But the other two heirs were deeply committed, with mortgages. I was the only one poor but free.

"Take it, Bevs!" Dick said on the phone.

"Well, I'll bring home pictures," I demurred, but the gleaming sun on Hidden Cove was pretty insistent.

The timing for a move was right. Peter was ready to graduate from eighth grade. We shuddered to remember his experience in public school and thought a suburban high school might be the answer. Dick and I were sure we could find jobs in Seattle and commute across Puget Sound by ferry.

So in 1977 we drove our yellow Datsun up to our new life in the country. We squeezed into Aunt Ted's summer cottage, found a local talented, but demanding carpenter, Bob Rockwell, and almost immediately added two rooms. I spent most of that first year going back and forth to Lumberman's getting or returning "18 12-penny nails" or "12 18-penny nails," as well as "two by fours" or "two by sixes," paint thinner, and the ground walnut shells Mr. Rockwell spread to keep the deck less slippery. Yes—except for that first weekend on the island—it rained almost every day.

Dick and I were able to find jobs, though not always to our liking. The kids' public schools were acceptable, and easier than Cathedral. Both boys loved the expansive woods behind our house. Dark, curly-haired Peter and his friend, Hutch Araki, ran around in black clothes and masks, pretending they were invisible.

Peter also began writing poetry. His poem "Slipping Away" won the Washington Poet's Association Totem Award, which was a surprise because I wasn't aware he had an interest in poetry—he was more into science fiction novels and comics—and it turned out the only reason he was up for the award was that his English teacher thought the poem had potential and sent it in. But first born Peter has always thrived on attention and he became a dedicated poet, attending adult poetry workshops on the island, often writing a full-page poem an hour before class. He became quite opinionated about what constituted a "decent poem" and placed in several more competitions in the coming years.

Blond Mark was more conservative, studying debate and wearing a tie like a grown-up lawyer. He was competitive, wanted to go out for football, but Dick and I said absolutely not—sturdy as he was, we didn't want him hurt. So he became a debater and later won two college national debate championships.

Peter began making movies with his friend Jeff Pedersen and filled our storage unit and yard with plastic buildings, stars, zombies, and action figures.

(Both Peter and Jeff are filmmakers in Los Angeles now. Peter makes documentaries for glass artist Dale Chihuly, and for other artists as well. Mark is an anthropologist and lawyer with posts in Bulgaria, Cambodia and Burma.)

Bainbridge being an artistic community, I soon enrolled in Bob McAllister's poetry class, an Olympic College Extension course at the high school. Occasionally, as time went on, Peter would be in the same adult class I took.

"Poetry is stupid," Dick said, half-kidding, until he began reading Charles Bukowski and Li Po. Then he changed his attitude, joined the class himself, and became an outstanding, widely-published poet. He gave readings at Elliot Bay Book Company in Seattle and Eagle Harbor Books on Bainbridge, and published three poetry books, *The Girl in the Albergo Borghese*, *The Woman in the Kettle of Fish* and *Cantos and Stories*. His "Great American Novel" continued to be rejected.

My first ESL job on the island was a class at Olympic College Extension in a church hall, St. Barnabas. I had to have 12 students, but an absolute minimum of 10 or the class would close. I had frequent conversations with my terrifying boss, Mr. Hatfield, who, if I didn't get the forms in on time, would cancel my class and yell at me on the phone. The students, often new Vietnamese refugees, might not show up the first day, so my registration lists usually included a janitor, a husband and at least one illegible completely-fictitious person.

A year later, I met Rachel Hidaka, a widely respected dean from Seattle Central Community College, at a statewide faculty conference.

"You have a Master's in ESL? I could use someone like you," she said. So for the next 30 years I commuted to a lively, varied, big-city job in the Central District of Seattle. No attendance problems and my dean never raised her voice. It took a few years before I realized that Mother, who grew up in Seattle at the turn of the century, had attended Broadway High School in the same building 70 years earlier.

In the 80s, while Peter and Mark were in high school, I kept up my poetry, wrote some short fiction for Nancy Rekow's local workshops and self-published a little book of both called *For All the Wrong Reasons*. The boys were out of the house a lot, on bikes or—ugh—in my car, so I had more time than when they were little.

Although Paris had been relegated to the very back portion of my mind, in the early 90s I discovered a little French group on the island. On Wednesday afternoons we'd drink tea or wine and speak French. So I always rushed back from Seattle on Wednesdays—Paris was still there.

At the Palace of the Legion of Honor, San Francisco

The Newlyweds!

Dick with Peter & Mark at Crissy Beach in San Francisco

Ralph Lehman, Bev's father

Part III

Back to Paris
with a
Backpack & Hair Dye

1993-Present

Hôtel des Académies ★ NN

Direction : FALABRÈGUE - CHARLES

15, Rue de la Grande Chaumière - 75006 Paris

Métro : Vavin - Raspail - Notre-Dame des Champs - Port Royal

TOUT LE CONFORT

DOUCHE - W.C. PRIVÉS - TÉLÉVISION

PARKING à proximité

Tél. : 01 43 26 66 44
Fax : 01 43 26 03 72
EURL AU CAPITAL de 8 000 €
SIRET N° 441 506 672 00019

M. West _____ ches

Adresse _____ Le 24 Sept

MOIS DE	du 9 au	25/09	
REPORT			
I CHAMBRE 16 N	68		1088 —
PETIT DÉJEUNER			
TÉLÉPHONE	54 90		54 90
4 café seul			20 —
TOTAL			1162 90
A REPORTER			

TOTAL GÉNÉRAL	1162,90

TAXES ET SERVICES COMPRIS

Hotel where the non-millionaires stay

29

Wake-up Call & Return to Paris

1993

It was only indigestion—those bands tight around my chest. But it sure *seemed* like a heart attack.

I shouldn't have had that margarita on an empty stomach. Shirley's mother had died after a long bout with cancer; Shirley'd phoned me to come over. Her son Kurt had handed me the icy margarita rimmed with crisp salt, and we'd sat around talking about our families, our careers—kind of like a wake.

Shirley was a sculptor and potter and I, in my heart, a writer, but we were both instructors now. Shirley helped kids make pots and figurines at Bainbridge Parks & Recreation District, while I modeled pronunciation and corrected papers at Seattle Central Community College. I loved working with students from Asia, Mexico and Europe, but what about my stories and poems—and maybe a book? Shirley and I were teaching, not *doing*.

Kurt was contentedly working as a decorator, and my kids were also doing their things—Peter a filmmaker, with a baby on the way, and Mark, in long hair and sandals, trekking to India for his law school thesis. I was glad for them, but now, what about me?

The death of Shirley's mother wasn't particularly sad; it had been expected and was, to Shirley and her husband, now watching TV in another room, really a relief.

"Would you like something to eat?" southern Shirley asked.

"No, I'm fine." I wasn't, hadn't had dinner, but didn't want to trouble her.

Another margarita and talk. Finally I left and drove home. Dick—always able to fend for himself—had fixed spaghetti and there was still some cold in the saucepan: swimming in tomato sauce, which I find too acidic, even without a queasy stomach.

"It's good. Try some," he said.

I decided I should eat something. I didn't bother to heat it up—just ate a few forkfuls after scraping off the tomato sauce. What I really needed was not food, but to get under the cool sheets, the warm blankets. Soon I lay back in bed, being still and meditating to calm my stomach. But it didn't work. In fact, I felt tight bands around my chest and getting tighter.

"Dick, call 911—hurry!" He did, and rushed down the stairs, two at a time, to open the front door and watch for the aid car.

Soon sirens screaming. Aid car driving up. Lights flashing. Kids younger than Peter and Mark—one with a nose ring, another with a mullet hairstyle—telling me what to do. How would they know?

"Sit on the chair, lady. We'll carry you down."

"Put this under your tongue." A small, white pill. "It'll dissolve."

Harrison Hospital—waiting, waiting—then a treadmill test. Soon, as they say in the newspapers, "treated and released."

A scare, a wake-up call. What do I want to do with my life? Are family and teaching enough? What happened to Europe? I'd lived in Paris as a student in the 50s, 35 years before, and had always planned to go back—next year, in two years….

The day Spring Quarter ended, I cashed in an IRA, bought a new green backpack and a ticket on Air Hitch—my younger, hippie son's way of travel. It was cheap, only $200 or so, based on overbooking. But you had to be willing to go to any one of four cities in your chosen area—in my case, Paris, Amsterdam, Berlin or London. The Air Hitch agent told me my destination was to be Amsterdam. After a restaurant dinner and one night there, I would "hitch" my way to Paris by train.

I had no idea how much Europe would cost. Traveling in the summer would probably be expensive. But I'd do it anyway—remember the chest pains and the treadmill!

Paris was the most important part of that trip to me and I knew I wanted to stay in a small hotel on the Left Bank, as I'd done in the 50s. A guidebook, *Cheap Sleeps in Paris,* offered lots of suggestions. One intrigued me: "Where Do All the Non-Millionaires Stay?"

It said Hôtel des Académies, in Montparnasse, near the Café Dôme. While preparing for my trip I phoned and made a reservation in my stumbling French, comforted to have a place to stay the first night in Paris.

Dick and our older son Peter took me to the airport on a late June afternoon, via REI and the purchase of some sturdy black walking shoes. My heavy cotton Hmong jacket, made by families of some of my students, with its purple and blue appliqué and cross stitching, would go anywhere—museums, restaurants, summer drizzle.

In Amsterdam I ate a gourmet Indonesian dinner, called a Rice Table, with many tiny spicy dishes and more young servers than I'd ever seen in one room. A waiter, talking to me as if I were an attractive woman and not, as in the US, an invisible 65-year-old, handed me my check on a carved brass plate and recommended a nearby hotel, a sort of ordinary, moderately-priced Holiday Inn Express. The next morning, excited, I took a train for Paris and my favorite area—noisy, student-filled Montparnasse.

Hôtel des Académies turned out to be a walk-up hotel, clean, with my own shower and toilet. More important, if I put my head out the window at just the right angle on a clear day and looked up the rue de la Grande Chaumière to the Boulevard Montparnasse, I could see the famous Café Dôme where, as a young expat, I'd spent many hours writing in my notebook.

This first morning, I would walk across the Grande Chaumière, past the familiar flower shop, and bend to put my face into the irises—deep blue, purple and mauve—and admire the orchids and Birds of Paradise. Then I'd amble down the Boulevard Raspail to the Alliance Française for a conversation class. Same walk, same language school I'd gone to in the 50s.

After registering at the Alliance, and maybe taking a placement test, I'd take a métro to Odéon and visit the now-famous Shakespeare & Co. bookstore, written up in all the guidebooks. I remembered meeting the proprietor, George Whitman, at the very same bookstore, then unknown and called The Mistral, at the same address, 37 rue de la Bûcherie. I wondered if George would remember me and perhaps let me read at one of his Monday nights. I'd brought along my chapbook of poems, *For All the Wrong Reasons,* and Dick's, *The Girl in the Albergo Borghese.*

In Europe, I was not just a newly visible woman again—but a writer. Coming back was the right move.

That was 1993 and I've managed—with a pack on my back—to get to Europe every year or so since, usually alone, once with a husband, once with a son, and in 2012, at 84, with my white-haired, ex-sailor boyfriend.

A Perfect Gentleman
1993

I'd loved him for all the wrong reasons,
his elusiveness, his Oxford accent—
this man I'd known so long ago—
now meeting again in Paris.

Anna, my traveling friend,
handed me free little cognacs from the plane,
"Have these with him," she said.
"You don't know what might happen."

I knew: Nothing would. Absolutely nothing.
Years before, I'd thought it was shyness,
though part of me already knew.

Now he waited in the Ritz lobby,
kissed me on both cheeks.
"*Un peu de France*," he smiled.

Quietly, he corrected my French.
But he was wrong;
he hadn't really heard
what I'd said to the waiter.

Still that night at the party I was proud of him.
He could talk about anything—
French wines, Chagal.

The Texas widow was fascinated.
"He wanted to see you again after 40 years—
He's so elegant.
Men are not like that any more.

"What will happen?"
She wanted to know.
"Nothing," I said.

"Impossible!" the widow said.
"After all, this is Paris—Gay Paree."

I couldn't tell her.

Dodging the Same Old Taxicab

Paris 1994

That morning I got up late and walked up the rue de la Grande Chaumière, past the flower shop to the Rotonde for a bowl of coffee with milk and a crusty tartine. There I perched on a stool at the zinc bar before heading to the Alliance Française on the Boulevard Raspail for the conversation class I'd enrolled in three weeks earlier. The zinc bar was quicker and cheaper than a table, I knew.

Of course nothing is quick in Paris and I savored the café crème into which I dipped the buttered bread. I looked at the headlines in the *International Herald Tribune* I'd bought at the large kiosk that carried foreign papers. Funny—same paper stand I'd gone to in the 50s. Same newspaper, but Art Buchwald, who used to be in the Paris office, now wrote his humor column—and books—from a cushy, unromantic office in New York.

Now I'd enrolled in the same language school, the Alliance Française, that I'd attended in the 50s and visited on my first trip back, the previous year. The better my French, the more fun I'd have in Paris. Back in the 50s, though, I'd mainly wanted to improve my French to be admitted into the Sorbonne.

I paid for my breakfast, which those days—the 90s—always included 15% service; I left an extra franc on the white ceramic dish, and got a gracious smile from the waiter. In 1952, before devaluation, a franc wasn't worth picking up off the ground, as my thrifty friend, John, used to say, and you'd certainly never leave one for a tip.

Leaving the café, I walked carefully past an open trap door where lettuce and corn were stacked on a dumbwaiter, and two waiters, a deliveryman and the *patron* (boss) were having an animated conversation. I watched the load disappear into the cave and the shelf reappear for its next load, cartons of bottled water that had been left on the side.

On Boulevard Montparnasse I signaled to the driver of the first taxi in the lineup. "150 Boulevard Raspail, *s'il vous plaît*." In the old days, I'd never have taken a taxi to a class five or six blocks away; usually only used them for moving my trunk to a different pension or hotel. But these days a month was a month, not an extended three years, and I wanted to savor it, taxi and all.

The teacher of that 10:30 conversation class was Corinne de Andreis—animated, slim and chic. She twirled to and from the blackboard, writing out new words on the board, blue pleated skirt moving around her. She lived in the suburbs of Paris as did most married couples. Fifty percent of Paris apartments were lived in by single people who'd inherited them, she told us. Out in the suburbs, the air was pure, unlike here in Paris with fumes from the taxis and buses and single-passenger cars.

Our class was multi-lingual, like those I taught in Seattle, and I got some ideas from her method, such as repeating an inaudible response from a quiet, reticent student and also writing it on the board. "The other students don't understand what the quiet Japanese students are saying," she said, "and this gives everyone something to write and take away with them."

Each of us had a turn to talk about a topic suggested earlier by the students. Today's was pollution and how it's handled in different countries. The Mexican doctor said that in Mexico their cars were marked to be used only on alternate days. He shrugged, "What do you do? I have more than one car, of course."

When it was my turn, I mentioned my job sharing with another teacher, so that I just rode the ferry into Seattle twice a week, which saved gas.

Small, dark-haired Emily Kisber came in late, *"Je m'excuse, Madame. Le bus était en retard."* (I'm sorry. The bus was late.) She spoke in a slow, southern drawl. She was my best friend at the Alliance Française; both of us in our sixties. *"Le Troisième Âge,"* (The Third Age) the French called it, honoring us with discounts on trains, métros and at museums. Both in love with Paris, we tried to speak French with each other. She used *"vous"* so I did, though I used the familiar *"tu"* with the younger students.

We took a couple of cooking classes at the Cordon Bleu on rue Léon Delhomme—me just for the experience, and Emily probably really to learn some gourmet tricks. The classes were helpful for our vocabulary because the lectures were translated, after each segment, from French to English.

Emily was gregarious, partly because she came from Atlanta, I guessed. With a daughter who worked for an airline, she could fly standby to Paris whenever she wanted. "Every family should have one child in the airline industry, as the Catholics used to do with the priesthood," I told her.

In America she worked as a lecturer for Weight Watchers, but when she wanted to travel, she could easily get a substitute. When we went to lunch, she asked for salad dressing on the side so she could just dip her fork in it and not get too much. And for a sandwich, she'd always say, *"Sans beurre,"* (without butter)—hard for me to copy since I loved butter on French bread.

Emily, an expert on buses, convinced me to buy a bus route book and use it. She also lectured tourists on how to use the bus. This was about the time of the métro bombings, when many tourists were afraid to go underground so took buses instead. Buses in Paris are never as easy as the infallible métro, but it's always wonderful to be aboveground in this historic city. One day, on a bus, we passed an eight-story building with wrought-iron balconies, which was being gutted, with the facade carefully boarded up and preserved. "No one will ever know about that from the outside; that's how they keep Paris beautiful," Emily told me.

Previously, Emily's husband had always come with her to Paris, but two years earlier he had been shot to death in his office, a mail order business in Atlanta that they'd operated together. Fifteen minutes later, he'd been found by a salesman. A young policeman came to the house to tell her. "He was so sweet," she said. "Wouldn't leave me until someone else came."

Emily ran the business for a year after that to see if she could find any reason why someone had killed him. But everyone seemed to like him, she said. So it might have been a random killing. Finally she gave up and sold the business with the murder still unsolved. She had lots of friends and dated occasionally, but said to me: "I'll always be lonely."

Most afternoons after class, Emily and I would have lunch at an outdoor café called Le Cassette, on the rue de Rennes—a *Salade Niçoise* with cheese, olives, tomatoes, and of course a *baguette—sans beurre*. With lunch we drank a glass of red house wine and finished off with a small, dark coffee. Emily tore open a slim packet of powdered sweetener and let it slide into her coffee. She was so used to doing this, and mentally counting calories, that it never occurred to her not to.

One afternoon we walked to St. Germain-des-Prés to look at shoes—for me—at the famous Arche store, where their sponge soles were so comfortable I felt justified in spending the hundred-plus dollars. After that we went to the *Musée Delacroix*, 6 rue de Furstenberg, one of the most charming squares in Paris where I'd always loved to sit and write—whether or not the tall, round lamps were lit. Sometimes I picnicked on fruit and cheese from a nearby delicatessen. The tiny museum there was Eugene Delacroix's former studio. We saw some of his drawings and paintings, then descended the narrow metal stairs to sit in a quiet garden—seemingly many kilometers away from busy Paris.

Later we went to rue de Paradis, the china and glass street where Emily wanted to buy some gifts. China shopping is boring for me, but I liked being with Emily. Soon, however, I left her shopping and took a bus she suggested to Place St. Michel. There I planned to see George Whitman at Shakespeare & Co. and ask about giving a reading—of my poems and Dick's—at one of his Monday evening gatherings.

Bev being fed after a class at the Cordon Bleu

Shakespeare & Co.

1994

A reading at Shakespeare & Co.—it would be something to tell my grandchildren. Maybe I could pull it off.

I felt 24 again and giddy to be in the Latin Quarter—though Paris was different now, with high prices and couples talking on cell phones as they walked. Sometimes—perhaps because it was Paris and they too were under its influence—they would stop to kiss.

I stopped for a large, steaming café au lait under a white umbrella at Le Petit Chatelet café next door to Shakespeare & Co. I wanted to compose myself before talking to George Whitman. It was a sweet, warm afternoon and I sat at a round, metal-rimmed table on the uncovered terrace, which in such weather, extended out onto the sidewalk. I wrote a few sentences in my notebook about the birds perched in the trees singing, the bells tolling from nearby Notre Dame and the headwaiter, in a black suit and bow tie, who rushed around shaking hands with the regular customers.

Then I called for my bill, "*Garçon, l'addition, s'il vous plaît.*" The tall, slim waiter, a long white apron over his black pants and vest, placed the bill on a saucer, "*Voila, Madame.*"

Some expatriates contend it's improper and demeaning to use the time-honored term, "*Garçon*" (boy), and instead call the waiter "*Monsieur.*" But French people have told me "garçon" is the job title and that it's perfectly correct. So when I'm with expats I say "Monsieur" and when alone or with the French, the more cool "Garçon."

Leaving some coins in the saucer, I walked over to the bright yellow Shakespeare & Co. sign stretched across the top of the bookshop windows.

On that soft, sunny afternoon, people were standing around outside the quaint red, yellow, and green shop front, looking at the bargains that a slight, white-haired George and his student-tenants had placed on long boards and tables in front. George himself was inside, perched at the horseshoe shaped counter, selling books.

I knew that George was now a fixture among the English-speaking writers and students. He'd let them cram their sleeping bags in nooks between bookcases and stay as long as they needed. The only charge was helping out a little and reading "a book a day."

I had first met George back in 1953 when, with an inheritance, he opened the bookshop—then called the Mistral, named for the famously fierce wind that blows through the south of France. When I first walked into the Mistral a soft-spoken young man with a crooked blond haircut offered me a cup of coffee, and then we sat on a cot and talked. I shyly.

The original Shakespeare & Co., on the rue de l'Odéon, had been run as a lending library in the days before World War II by an American book lover, Sylvia Beach. Her clientele included Hemingway, Kay Boyle, Scott Fitzgerald and Gertrude Stein. It was probably best known as the publishing house where Beach bravely typed and printed *Ulysses*, risking jail and fines for obscenity. Later, after Sylvia Beach died on October 5, 1962, George Whitman honored her memory by renaming his bookshop, at 37 rue de la Bûcherie—and also his daughter—after her, Sylvia Beach Whitman.

Now George's bookshop, run by his daughter, is open from 10 a.m. to 11 p.m. every day of the week. Sylvia Whitman follows her father's custom of encouraging lengthy browsing—one can sometimes read an entire book in an afternoon. Upstairs in the library, there are many familiar titles: English and American classics by Somerset Maugham and Henry James; *Justine* and other novels by Lawrence Durrell, Thomas Hardy, Henry Fielding, William Thackery, Bram Stocker of *Dracula* fame, Anthony Trollope, James Boswell, James Fenimore Cooper of *The Last of the Mohicans*, Ralph Waldo Emerson, Nathanial Hawthorne, Melville (*Moby Dick, Typee,* etc.), Thoreau, Poe, Mark Twain, Keats, Shelley, and also children's books like *Heidi* and *The Secret Garden*. Writers and tourists are likely to say to each other, "I'll meet you at Shakespeare."

George had a sign on the wall: "Be not inhospitable to strangers lest they be angels in disguise." I knew that was his philosophy, and why he let students and writers stay at the bookstore for long periods—sometimes months. I hoped he'd be hospitable to *me*—I'd brought my book of poetry to Paris and planned to show it to him.

Already there were early browsers inside the bookshop. I walked in, scanned the front shelves, and picked out something to buy— Hemingway's *A Moveable Feast*, which I decided had to be reread while in Paris. When George was less busy I'd talk to him, ask about giving a reading, and if I could leave a few of my own books to sell.

"Hi, George. Is this the right amount?" I held out the paperback and a 100 franc note.

"Yes. Everyone's favorite book. I can't keep it in stock." Then I wanted to snatch it back and select something more original, but he'd already taken my money and stamped the Shakespeare picture on the title page, pushed a couple of buttons on an adding machine, and stuffed the money into a cardboard shoebox.

"You were here last year. You're a writer."

"Well, yes. I'm Beverley West. I brought my poetry book. Maybe later you'd like to look at it…maybe stock it here." From my bag I pulled out a copy of *For All the Wrong Reasons* and handed the square red volume to him. I'd self-published it, had Nancy Rekow edit and proofread it and Elizabeth Zwick design it. For the cover, I'd used a drawing by artist Michelle Van Slyke. I thought it looked wonderful.

George put the top on the shoebox, and the line of people waited while he read through a few of the first poems. I shifted my feet from side to side, front to back, and tried not to look at him. Suppose he thought they were awful and said so out loud? He squinted, drooled a little, then took the book over to the window, and turned a few more pages. He said:

"They're good. You can have a reading here. That's the way to sell them."

A reading at Shakespeare & Co! All part of the mystique of Paris. But I had to remind myself of the reality—this wasn't Sylvia Beach's bookshop; James Joyce's *Ulysses* hadn't been published here; it was just another store by the same name. I knew I was being seduced by Paris and this wizened bookseller, with the Seine and gothic Notre Dame right there participating.

"Two weeks from Monday night is free," George said. "Come for dinner first. I always make ice cream."

"That sounds wonderful," I said. The book buyers in line kept busy—reading bits from the books they were buying or from others on George's table.

Deciding to check out the library, where the readings sometimes were held, I climbed up the narrowest, steepest stairs I'd ever been on and found myself in a room with books stacked from floor to ceiling, sleeping bags stuffed under cots, and—good grief— cockroaches the size of door knobs in one corner. Still, near the front windows, a reading would be possible here. Some of the books were tempting. I opened Proust's *Remembrance of Things Past*—suitable for reading in Paris—and several one-thousand-franc bills fell out onto the worn red carpet.

"Oh!" I picked a few up.

"George puts money in books for safekeeping," laughed a plump young man, reading on a corner stool, "but he forgets how much and where he put it." I stuck the notes back and, a little uncomfortably, reshelved Proust. I read from a few more paperbacks, losing myself in the bookshop. Then I walked to the tiny, cramped kitchen next door, where in front of a cracked mirror stood George, candle in hand, "cutting" his hair.

"Let me help you," I said, pulling out a pair of nail scissors from a cosmetics case in my pack. "I sneaked these through security. You could burn yourself."

"Go away. I've been doing this for years," he turned toward me, and said, rather ferociously for a soft-voiced man, "What are you? Rockefeller?—waste money on haircuts—and dye too, I think."

He blew out the candle and placed a thin, wrinkled hand shakily on my head, eyeing my roots: grey beneath the youthful—I was sure—auburn. "I can't see very well," he said.

Then, apparently forgetting the roots, he leaned closer and said, "You say you're a writer, well, you have to cut down—no restaurants or bars. I buy food at the street markets just before they close—they almost give it away. I'll show you tomorrow, if you stay here.

"Now go away. Let me get on with this!" He took out another match from a box on the counter and relit the candle.

Stay at the bookshop? Certainly not in the library. However, I did stay that night, just for the experience and a sentence or two in my notebook. George gave me a small bedroom with red wallpaper on which there were pictures of writers, including a poster-size one of Hemingway.

Next morning I went over to a print shop on Boulevard St. Germain and copied the title page of my book in order to make a sign. There was enough white space at the bottom to print the date, time and famous location in ink. I borrowed scissors, White Out and rubber cement from the attendant, cut and pasted until I thought it looked right, then ran off 10 copies to tack up in the lobby of my hotel, on the bulletin board in the downstairs hall at the Alliance Française, and at the Village Voice and a few other bookstores.

Back at Shakespeare & Co., I reached up the outside bulletin board to thumbtack the first of my signs. But there were already signs up for another reading that same Monday night. George was calm, "I forgot Israel Halpern is reading that night. But you can read with him....His friends are going to videotape it. There they all are— out on the bench."

Looking through the glass, I saw a man with a long, black beard peeling an orange and two other men in sweaters, jeans and sneakers, one talking excitedly. I walked over. "Hi, I'm Beverley." I showed them a copy of the advertisement of my reading—with the same date as theirs. The bearded man was Israel, a college instructor who told me he taught prisoners in New York jails.

He offered me a section of his orange. "I think George got confused and signed us both up for the same night," he said. "But sure, we can read together. In fact, we'll send you a copy of the video."

The night of the reading there were soft breezes. I arrived early, but George was nowhere in sight. Must have forgotten he'd invited me for dinner. I had an apple in my pack, which I ate while Israel and his friends set up the microphones and wooden chairs facing the bookshop where we stood and read alternately. The audience included some people I'd seen at Shakespeare as well as Emily, a few other Alliance students, and even Cyd, my hotel manager. In the back I saw the Beat poet Ted Joans with his artist girlfriend, Laura Corsiglia. We read as the sun set, but illumination from the nearby stately Notre Dame Cathedral gave us enough light to read by.

Israel read several poems about teaching in New York jails. I read some of Dick's humorous pieces set in bars, and from my book my own poems about marriage and teaching ESL.

They seemed to like us. "At least they laughed and clapped in the right places," Israel said. Later I found out the microphone had worked less than half the time.

"Why did you stay if you couldn't hear?" I asked an elderly English couple I'd seen at the bookshop.

"Because it's Paris," the slender, white-haired woman answered. "There's nothing like Notre Dame when it's lit up—the light reaches all the way to Shakespeare. That's poetry enough." Actually I now have a videotape of the reading that Israel sent me. So I can hear our voices and see our images against the famous yellow sign of Shakespeare & Co.

Bev and friend at Shakespeare & Co. for Sunday tea

A reading at Shakespeare & Co. Bev, seated, in black strapped sandals

Paris with Dick & Farewell to Princess Di

August, 1997

"Remember your promise, Bevs—not to take too much." Dick, slim and graying, walked into our room and stood over the bed, eyeing my open bag along with piles of shirts, slacks, jeans, sandals, sweaters, and a purse or two.

Finally, our first trip to Paris together, after 32 years of marriage.

I wanted everything to go smoothly, so extracted some sandals and an extra purse.

We'd decided to take matching travel bags, so we'd gone together to a local store, The Traveler, and selected Rick Steeves bags—Dick's green and mine Merlot—with handles for carrying and also straps so we could use them as backpacks. Only thing missing was WHEELS. And, yes, I realized later, I *had* packed too much. So I vowed, on my next trip, to take a carry-on with wheels.

We didn't have to worry about packing our poetry books. When I'd told George Whitman of Shakespeare & Co. about Dick, and had read a couple of Dick's poems at Israel's and my reading, George had invited us both to read at his bookstore.

"Not bad—a reading in Paris," Dick had said, giving me a hug.

We'd each mailed 10 of our books to the hotel, so we could sell a couple at the reading, give some to friends, and still leave a few for George Whitman to sell—maybe—for us.

Despite an hour's delay at Sea-Tac, our flight to Paris went smoothly. I'd bought elastic stockings for 25 dollars to keep my ankles from swelling, and we walked up and down the aisle as often as we could without being too conspicuous. I also did stretching exercises in an enclosure behind the lavatory. So we were in pretty good shape when we got off the plane.

The Hôtel des Académies was waiting for us, clean and cheap as ever, and Cyd, the wide-smiled Cape Verdean manager, handed us our packages of books as we reached the top of the steps to the little second-floor lobby. He and an assistant carried our bags up to the small, yellow-wallpapered room—one of the "luxury" rooms—with its own shower.

"Is it OK, Dick?" I asked hesitantly. Lots of people didn't agree with my backpack-style travel economy. "Look out the window—up to the left is the Café Dôme!"

"It's fine," he said, looking out the window. "Let's sign in and give the Dôme a try."

Dick and I, jacketless in August, ambled up to Boulevard Montparnasse and settled at a round wicker table on the Dôme terrace. I delighted in the sweet, warm air, knowing the white-aproned waiters might put up glass partitions if it cooled off later in the evening.

A tall, dark-haired waiter came over, *"Monsieur/Dame."* I was proud of the way Dick handled the situation, with a quiet "May I speak English?" rather than asking "Do you....?" This method, which we'd learned from our traveler son Mark, assumes the person you're talking to is educated, capable, and certainly knows English.

The waiter, who catered to tourists daily, of course spoke English, so Dick proceeded to order. Usually a two-or-three-Martini man, he asked for grenadine and a glass of mineral water, while I had a glass of burgundy. I was amazed at his choice—had rather worried that the Martinis would strain our budget—but wanted Paris to be a joy for both of us, so had planned to go along with whatever he needed to do. Not so perfect myself, I must admit we'd both gotten sloshed at the Seattle airport, had a couple of doubles when our plane was a little delayed. Actually it turned out Dick drank no alcohol the entire month we were in Paris. "Grenadine is very French and really hits the spot—and I know Paris is going to be expensive," he explained on our third or fourth day.

From our table, we could look across the boulevard to the Café Select and the illuminated statue of Rodin's Balzac. I shifted my chair a little to see the statue better.

Finishing our drinks, it was getting toward 7 p.m. "How about dinner?" I asked.

"Let's try the restaurant you're always talking about—the Beaux-Arts."

"Are you game to walk?" I asked.

"You know I am." Dick was an avid runner. In fact, in the 60s in San Francisco, he'd been one of the first regular runners and had a hard time finding sweats in the men's departments. So now, with his long legs, a walk was easy for him.

"Let's get our bill." Dick lifted his glass to finish the pomegranate cordial syrup.

The Dôme waiter hovered a few tables away. *"L'addition, s'il vous plaît,"* I said without thinking and the waiter put the bill on a saucer next to my glass rather than Dick's. But it didn't really matter which of us paid as it was "all out of the same pocket" as my father used to say. We counted up the check, and the service was included. Dick put the bills on the saucer and I suggested we leave an extra 10 francs, which he did.

As we walked up to the Beaux-Arts, near St.-Germain-des-Prés, I had Dick practice *"L'addition, s'il vous plaît"* until he got it perfect. "I'll try it out at the restaurant," he said.

"You could pass for a Frenchman, with your olive skin and, now, a perfect French phrase," I told him. Still good-looking at 70, I thought.

Except for a new paint job, the Beaux Arts was the same crowded, bustling place where my parents, sister and I had indulged ourselves nearly every evening in 1953. Back then, in my 20s, I'd had the sauces the French are famous for and frequently ended a meal with a *Mont Blanc—fromage blanc* and pureed chestnuts. Now Dick and I decided on fish with a white cream sauce, cauliflower *au gratin* (baked with grated cheese on top), salad, and ended up with a *Mont Blanc*, though it wasn't on the menu and I had to explain it to the waiter. The restaurant was so crowded and confused that Dick was content to have me, with my French, deal with the waiter, and the bill and get back out in the air.

On our walk home, I pointed out the little organic restaurant, the Dietetic Shop, I liked on rue Delambre. Dick looked in the window at the counter and booths and spent a long time studying the handwritten menu, with drawings of the foods, taped on the glass door.

"We could try it sometime. We're semi-vegetarians," he said.

That night we started out sleeplessly, both with slight stomachaches. "We're not 24," Dick said. "Enough *Mont Blancs* for me!"

"OK, OK." I rubbed my stomach and took a deep breath, "The Dietetic Shop tomorrow." That decision made, we each fell into a deep sleep.

One of Paris's main charms is its food, so after sightseeing and visiting bookstores and museums, we got in the habit of ending our day with a gourmet—but vegetarian and organic—meal at that same little shop behind the Dôme on rue Delambre.

There we'd squeeze ourselves into a narrow booth, equipped with a tray of condiments—green oil, soy, salt, pepper, garlic, yeast and the shop's own special seasoning salt. Outside there were two tables, tempting, with conversations from passersby and tolling from the church bells at St.-Germain-des-Prés. However, a nearby building was being torn down, which made eating outdoors noisy and dusty.

Even vegetarian food—lentils, boiled vegetables, freshly picked salad, and fruit tart—is gourmet in Paris. Frequently we chose a small carrot juice and *riz complet*—brown rice with tasty boiled beets, cabbage, turnips, carrots, and curls of black seaweed, my favorite part. We felt so good that Dick and I promised ourselves we'd eat this way at home and even buy a juicer—which we did after the trip, but didn't use all that much.

Another advantage to the Dietetic Shop: although we ordered in French—my department—the customer didn't pay the waiter. Dick would go up to the cashier and settle the bill as we left with the English-speaking cashier.

The next morning I would walk past the Rodin statue along Boulevard Raspail to my conversation class at the Alliance Française, then meet Dick, with his notebook, on a green wooden bench at the spacious, grassy, and flower-filled Luxembourg Gardens.

The Alliance, which I tried to attend whenever in Paris long enough, was much the same as in the 50s. There, teachers still wiped off the chalkboards with wet sponges from a bucket kept on a chair at the side. However, they also now had computer-generated handouts, similar to ours in the States. The students were of all ages and from many countries.

We had a good time together. We shopped in antique shops for a netsuke, a small carved ivory figurine used as a toggle on a traditional Japanese kimona, which Dick wanted to take home as a souvenir. We went to the usual museums, parks and cafés; attended Sunday tea with the wizened 90ish owner, George Whitman, upstairs at Shakespeare & Co. and, while there, put up signs for our reading. I spent part of each day walking around on my own, taking buses and practicing my French on anyone who would talk to me. It was a relief not to have to translate, yet always comfortable to know I'd be meeting Dick—for a drink on a café terrace with cathedral bells tolling and birds chirping on trees nearby, or for dinner at our special restaurant. My earlier summers, in the 90s, had been all French, but a little lonely.

Our reading at the bookstore on rue de la Bûcherie was upstairs in the library, well attended, with some of the same people who'd been to my reading with Israel Halpern in 1994. Again, as Israel had said, the audience was appreciative and "laughed in the right places." I read a few poems from my book, *For All the Wrong Reasons*, including a spoofing one about Dick's and my writing, which they liked.

Homage to Vera Nabokov

"Here's something for your wall," my husband says.
"Vera Nabokov's obituary." He tacks it to the corkboard.

"But that's right on top of the contest rules!
My limerick contest!" I take it off and give it back.

He waves the clipping in the air.
"An inspiration for you—a wonderful, dedicated life.
Look at all she did for her writer-husband—'wife, muse,
ideal reader, his secretary, typist, editor,
proofreader, translator and bibliographer....'"

"But I have my own typing to do," I say,
"and I do do your proofreading and editing."

"Look," he says, "there's more—'agent, manager,
legal counsel' and—look, right here—'chauffeur....'"
(Gosh, that's me! I wish he'd get a driver's license.)

"But I need time for my limericks—they're only five lines."

He tacks the obit up again.
"Well," he says, "try haiku. They're only three."

Dick read from his *Girl in the Albergo Borgese* and *Cantos &
Stories*. The audience roared when he ended with my favorite of his
titled "Einstein's Flowers:"

"What if, say, he'd gotten into painting..."—T.L.S.

When Albert Einstein was a young man
working for the patent office in Zurich
he decided to broaden his horizons
by enrolling in a basic watercolor class.

The instructor was a jovial little fellow
who arrived each Thursday evening
with a bowl of flowers for the students to copy
& as time passed the buxom lady with the braids
who sat at Einstein's right
showed marked improvement, as did the bald-headed
bank clerk at his left,
before long the whole class was making progress,
everyone except Einstein.

The kindly instructor tried to be helpful
by giving Einstein encouragement at each session
but as hard as Einstein tried
the bowls of pansies, poppies, geraniums, or daisies
always ended up looking like equations.

After a while Einstein lost interest in watercolor
& didn't come around anymore.

They clapped, demanding more. Dick read another 15 minutes, laughed and said, "I'm getting hoarse!"

Still, we didn't sell any books. "Don't worry," George said. "People who come to the readings don't have money with them. I'll stock some and sell them for you that way." True to his word, he'd already sold several before we left Paris.

But later there was real sadness in that Paris trip. We were there on August 31, 1997—a Sunday. We'd walked up the steps to the hotel lobby when Cyd stopped us, and said to me: *"La Princesse Diana est morte!"*

An accident. Her lover, Dodi, killed also. Cyd showed us the papers and had the TV on. Papers and TV were full of it: pictures of the beautiful, blonde Englishwoman in a white satin evening dress and tiara, in a bathing suit, in blue running clothes, one picture next to Dodi with his arm around her waist. The paparazzi who were to be blamed—vilified for their constant intrusions—had an embarrassing assortment of background pictures to choose from.

The horror of it—a drunken chauffeur racing through the Alma tunnel—his royal passenger suddenly battered from side to side against upholstery, glass and metal. Blood, pain, and, of course, flash bulbs.

I walked out to the kiosk in front of the Café Select and bought for myself the French evening paper, *Le Monde*, which I could read with the help of my pocket dictionary.

"There is no *Tribune* on Sunday, Madame. It will be here in the morning," the proprietor of the tiny round structure said in French. "I'll save you your two copies." Just to be sure, I paid her the 20 francs in advance so Dick and I would have our individual English-language newspapers with our coffee at the café the next morning.

We'd agreed that the *International Herald-Tribune* was better than most American newspapers. So, whether or not there was a major news story, we often indulged ourselves with a copy each, so we didn't have to say, "Are you finished with Page 3 yet?"

Next morning we read our newspapers with coffee and croissants at a round table at the Select. Usually our breakfasts had been happy occasions—we'd laugh about our problems with the language and plan what museum we'd go to or walk we'd take after my class. But our mood that morning was somber.

The accident continued to fill the papers, with pictures and quotes from English and French friends and from Diana's brother. Diana had been frank about her unfaithful husband and her struggles with bulimia, so these didn't seem just news stories to us, but rather details about the death of a friend.

At a nearby table, a cell phone rang. A bejeweled American woman was arranging for a guided tour. She spoke into her phone, a little loudly and quite distinctly:

"Yes, I want to see the Louvre, the Musée d'Orsay for the impressionist paintings. And—can you take me to the tunnel?"

***

In 2001, when we were both 74, Dick and I agreed to divorce— probably something most people wouldn't do at that age. But we're still friends. We attend each other's poetry readings on Bainbridge Island, and celebrate holidays and family birthdays together. We're both close to Peter and Mark, their wives and kids. Another constant in my life is that I've done my best to continue my trips—sometimes solo, sometimes not—to Paris.

Dick's first poetry book

Looking out from a favorite hotel

I could see Café Dôme from my window.

33

Paris in the Heat & Camping in Ireland

Summer, 2003

That summer of 2003, people my age in France were dying from the heat. Many families went away on vacation, leaving *Grandmère* in an upstairs apartment, weakened by the heat, unable to get to the kitchen for water and food. Although they called us *Le Troisième Âge,* (The Third Age), and honored us with discounts on trains, *métros* and museums, they hadn't prepared us for the high temperatures and terrible humidity.

The many deaths may have included Diana Mosley, 93, of the celebrated Mitford sisters who was the widow of Sir Oswald Mosley, leader of the British Union of Fascists. She had written to a friend 10 days before her stroke and death in her Paris apartment that she was finding the heat wave a struggle.

The newspapers were full of statistics and warned traveling families to check on their parents. The city of Paris should have done more, I felt. There were even stories about unidentified elderly people who had died and were being buried in unmarked graves.

Mark had flown to Paris to meet me and later explore Ireland, my grandparents' and his great-grandparents' birthplace. Now we would amble slowly from our Hôtel des Académies to the movie houses, with signs posted saying *climatisé* (air-conditioned) on the Boulevard Montparnasse, or for a drink of Cinzano or Perrier at the spacious, modernized Café Coupole. We always carried bottled water, refilled it in bathrooms or fountains, or bought more. Sometimes when I wasn't even thirsty, I made myself drink, and my headache or vacant feeling or dizziness would disappear.

We didn't stay in Paris very long, although it's my favorite place in the whole world and I forgive it all its famous faults—snobbery, high prices, rudeness. The heat didn't let up so we left for Ireland days before we'd planned. We took the "Chunnel" across the English Channel from Gare du Nord in Paris to London, stayed there long enough to have drinks and dinner with my old friend from Paris in the 50s, John Walton, and his partner since 1966, Roger Raglan.

Actually, they became civil partners two years after our visit, on December 21, 2005, the very first day it was legally possible to do so in England. "If I had 'come out' whilst still employed in Government, I would have lost my security clearance and so all prospect of a good career," John wrote me.

Mark and I then flew from London to Cork and stayed in a large hostel for a week or so. The climate was not unlike moist Bainbridge Island, so we breathed it in and relaxed. We went to theaters—in lilting but very understandable English—and a dance performance. We looked up Bolster—as both my maternal grandparents had the same name—in church and county records, but found little that was relevant. Mark rented a bike and came back saying "We *have* to go to the country. It's beautiful."

So we rented a small Ford and drove off the main highways. The first night we slept next to a crumbling castle in a little park called Carrigadrohid, just outside Cork in eastern Ireland, and swam in the moat before we left. But we couldn't have a castle every time.

Then we began camping in green fields—usually, but not always, after getting permission from the farmer owner. Our first such venture was easier for Mark than for me.

"No, I can't climb a barbed wire fence," I told him. "Besides, it's illegal. It's somebody's private field."

"Sure you can, Mom." He held his hands, stirrup style, for me to put my foot in. We'd parked our car in a wide spot by the road, leaving the backpacks, sleeping bags and tent inside, while we scouted for our night's lodging.

Actually, I didn't climb that particular fence. I felt safer crawling under it while Mark pulled up the bottom wires. My shirt and jeans got really dirty as I pressed against the dried mud. Crawling, at dusk, without getting cut by barbed wires, was a pretty good feat for a seventy-something senior and a non-athletic one at that. After I brushed myself off, we searched for an area with bushes that would hide our tent.

Even wearing hiking boots, we had to walk gingerly so as not to trip on the deep, hard hoofprints of cattle that had grazed there. We found a protected spot hidden from the road yet with a delightful view of green fields, tidy farms, and sheep in the distance.

"You wait here, Mom. I'll go back and get the stuff."

I'd planned to do my share of the carrying, but my legs and back felt stiff, so I decided to let him do it. "What a wonderful son!" I said. "I'm so lucky."

He laughed, "It's pay-back time."

I plunked myself down on a boulder and loosened my bootlaces a little. I leaned forward, rubbing my knees and my lower back. I'd gotten cramped in that little car. Mark jogged off toward the road, a good deal faster than we'd walked together. I realized I'd have to be sure he got some hikes by himself. The breeze felt cool against my cheek after the headachy heat of Paris.

Ireland was one of our main destinations, so we didn't mind giving it extra time. I hadn't been there since my student days in Europe and Mark never had. Because of our heritage, Ireland—and particularly Cork, where our forebears were born—was important to us both. I'd even gotten an Irish passport, allowable with an Irish grandparent, which meant I was an EU citizen.

Some 20 minutes after he'd left our campsite, I saw Mark in the distance, carrying two backpacks and also two sleeping bags, and two plastic ground covers—which after the cold earth of Carrigadrohid I'd insisted we buy. The tent was a little 40-Euro tent we'd found in downtown Cork. He also carried bottled water, bread, bananas, and extra socks. He'd tied some things onto himself and had his arms full of the remainder.

We set up the tent, which had three layers, including mosquito netting and a rainproof cover. The only problem was you had to unzip them all to get out in the middle of the night. At 35 you didn't have to; after 70 you did, and possibly more than once.

Those deep hoofprints extended even to our sleeping area. It was empty of livestock now, but the ground was hard and lumpy so the plastic ground covers made it possible to sleep. Our guidebook had listed a nearby campground, but it was pretty depressing, with campsites close together and radios fighting each other on different stations, so we drove in and right out again. After that, I agreed that fields were the only possible lodging.

The next night we did ask for permission. We parked our car and walked up to a farmer's wife in a striped shirt and straw hat who was pulling weeds in her flower garden. We talked a minute, then I said, "Do you think we could camp way over there in your field?"

"Yes, but my son has a better field. Ask him. His house is down that way." It turned out her son did have a better one—an expanse of green with a fairy fort that was not to be touched.

"See that circle of trees?" the freckle-faced son pointed at them in the distance. "They say fairies used to live there and maybe still do. Our family doesn't really believe in them," he said, "but we don't go near the circle just the same. We don't bother them, and they don't bother us." I'd heard about the "little people" from my grandmother, so I'm a half-believer myself.

The son's daughter, about 18 or 19 with curly blond hair and freckles on her face and arms, got into an old convertible and drove us partway up the emerald field, past a dozen lambs. "They won't bother you," she said as she waved goodbye, then turned around and drove back.

We hurried over to the fairy fort, of course, even before setting up the tent. We walked completely around it, looking at the earthen mounds and the evenly spaced trees. There are 30,000 to 40,000 of these forts throughout Ireland. We read that, during the famine, parish churches were abandoned and people were too weak to carry their dead very far. We wondered if some brought them to the fairy forts, and dug shallow graves.

Lying in our sleeping bags, Mark asked, "Do you miss Dad—miss being married?"

"I don't think so, Mark. We had many great years together, especially when you kids were growing up."

"I guess Dad wasn't a traveler. Was that part of it?

"Maybe," I said. I knew both Peter and Mark had been sad about the divorce three years before—both still remained loyal to their father—but they were grown now and had their own lives.

Next morning, after bananas and some bread, we carried our backpacks down to the car and then walked over to the woman's house to thank her.

"Come in," she said. "We'll have tea."

The whole family was there, except for the daughter. Breakfast was served in a tiny, very old room with a woodstove and a table where Mark and I sat, eating homemade bread with butter and plum jam. The grandfather smoked constantly with a pipe set right between his lower teeth. Other rooms had been built on, including the kitchen. But this was obviously the most important one and the oldest. We talked for a couple of hours and finally left, after getting addresses and promises that they would visit us.

Originally we'd planned to drive all the way to Northern Ireland and visit major tourist attractions on the way. But in one or two crowded places, with people pushing against each other while buying postcards, we almost tacitly decided to take the back roads, enjoy the scenery, and avoid the tourist spots. Farmers and their animals were enough for a while.

Traveling with a vegan was eye-opening. We had to inspect every menu and I became very much aware of which dishes had a little milk or cheese, which Mark couldn't have, in the sauce. When we stopped at a farm to look at the animals, I was really charmed to see families—cows, bulls, and calves—lick and fondle each other. In our country, on most factory farms they don't even know each other. I became a stricter vegetarian too, that summer.

It's hard to believe that a mother and grown son could travel together for five weeks. However, we did have several separations when we returned to Paris, so Mark could visit a friend and I could go alone to cafés to practice my French. Still, our basic philosophy was the same: traveling is the most important thing to do with your life and your salary. Mark knew that originally I had saved to go to Paris since I was nine.

"Money means tickets," he would still say.

Paris with White Hair and a New Boyfriend

September & October, 2011

It was taking a chance—going back to Europe and MY Paris with Bob, my white-haired, pony-tailed boyfriend who didn't even speak French! A retired librarian, he was slim with a long Gaelic nose and a mouth that smiled so seldom I had to really listen to catch his wry comments. But he was a good sport, a hearty walker, and enjoyed Paris too, so we survived.

Actually Bob had spent a few days in Paris in the 80s when he and his late wife had visited their son, who was there studying the flute. But in general his travels had taken him in other directions via the Merchant Marines.

Bob and I planned on a three-week trip, because my Paris friend Odette—who rented out an extra room in her apartment—had that exact amount of lax time between student tenants. We'd get the room plus laundry, maid service, and kitchen privileges at a *prix d'ami* (friend's price).

The most reasonable airfare was to Amsterdam. From there we would train trek to Paris, so we booked round-trip, non-refundable tickets. I waited till almost midnight—a decent morning hour in Paris—to call Odette, "It's all set!"

But she was silent for a minute. A long minute, then said *"Je suis désolée, tellement désolée"* (I'm terribly sorry). She didn't need to go on. Her fall student was arriving early and *had* to have the room right away.

"Mais, Odette. But, but"—there were tears in my voice. That

still didn't do any good. After more than three years in Paris, I'd learned—when the French make up their minds, no amount of American sweetness can change it.

So Bob and I made the best of it. First, though Paris was our main destination, we wouldn't short-change Amsterdam. My daughter-in-law, Zuzana, with youthful Internet acumen, found us a two-room houseboat on a canal. Heavenly! At breakfast we'd drop bread crusts out our window to squawking ducks and fat geese and then we'd walk or bus to town.

Everybody in Amsterdam was tall, slim, and athletic-looking, making me regret any day I'd missed going to the Fitness Center back home on Bainbridge. People of all ages were riding bikes, many carrying parcels or groceries in baskets, on their backs, or under their arms. We passed a 9,000-bicycle garage, the size of half a city block, wide open to view, with bikes crowded against each other—and a workman told us the huge garage was being enlarged!

That first day we went to the Rijksmuseum, which was being renovated—requiring us to walk through makeshift corridors to the obligatory 11' by 14' Rembrandt, "Night Watch." Its "mascot," a little girl with a strangely mature face, wore a golden dress and held a dead chicken and a pistol. The famous painting was too militant for my taste—I warmed to Vermeer's "Milkmaid" with her strong, capable arms—but "Night Watch" was of major importance to art lovers and to the Dutch. It was the only one in the gallery to have its own escape slide: a trapdoor allowing it to be quickly moved in case of fire or other calamity.

To reach the Anne Frank house, we bought tickets at a shoreline boarding dock for a boat ride along a canal, passing shops and houses and many one-story houseboats like our own. At the tall, narrow museum, we climbed steep steps to a large, dreary room where the adolescent girl had had to remain totally quiet for years or face a concentration camp. The house was unfurnished, as requested by one of the survivors, but we walked around and imagined where the Franks had cooked, eaten, studied, slept, and listened in terror for any unusual sound. In the gift shop I bought the *Diary of Anne Frank* that, amazingly, I had never read—then finished it in Paris. I was deeply moved by Anne's story, and found myself reading and rereading her book on buses or in a museum line.

On our last night in Amsterdam, the little houseboat rolled pleasantly with the waves as we went to sleep. Early in the morning I heard some quacking, reminding us of our breakfast duties. "I half-wish we could live on a boat on Bainbridge," I told Bob as I threw some crusts out to the quackers. I knew he'd spent much of his life on boats, first on Merchant Marine ships and then in the Caribbean on his own sailboats.

"It's a great life," he acknowledged, "but sunshine helps." (A commodity we lacked in the Pacific Northwest).

After packing, en route to the train station we passed an enormous outdoor market where bicyclists were buying food and clothing, which they stuffed into backpacks and baskets for their journeys home. Then to Paris by train. No matter how often I went there, I always gasped with delight at my first sight of the dark, busy people, cafés extending out onto the pavement, streetlamps lighting storefronts, wrought iron balconies, and the sweet, nasal sounds of the world's most beautiful language.

We took a cab to rue de la Tombe Issoire, where I'd been able to arrange a last-minute rental of a studio belonging to my Bainbridge artist friend, Michelle Van Slyke, where I'd stayed by myself on several earlier trips.

"Another apartment—I don't know," Bob had said as I made the arrangements after our first Paris flat fell through. "I'll believe it exists when we actually go through the door." It did and we did.

The studio was, as the French would say, *complet*—silverware and utensils in the tiny kitchenette, pullout beds, maps, guidebooks, telephone, and even a towel-warmer in the bathroom (handy for drying socks and underwear overnight, I remembered from a previous stay at Michelle's).

Bob, who loves to cook, opened kitchen drawers, cabinets, and the tiny oven door. "I can make do—but no turkey," he said.

We marketed nearby, economized by cooking many meals in the studio, but had coffee and croissants at the Café Select most mornings. I showed Bob the Paris I knew, including Shakespeare & Co., with the aged, dying, but sweetly smiling owner, George—who we climbed the wide, circular staircase to chat with.

Bob, who'd been a librarian for 25 years, knew about George from reading Jeremy Mercer's *Time Was Soft There*, an account of life at Shakespeare & Co. I loved the Mercer book, with stories about Mercer himself—one of the many writers or students George had let stay there for the usual price: "Help a bit and read a book a day." However, George himself did not like Mercer's book: "It's full of inaccuracies," he'd growled and refused to stock it.

When Bob and I walked into the bedroom, George raised himself on an elbow under his covers, looked at me hard and said he remembered me. I knew he really did because he put his free hand up to hide his haircut, since I'd always teased him after catching him that time in the kitchen "cutting" his hair by burning it with a candle.

I'd hoped to give a Monday poetry reading, but we learned that Sylvia Beach Whitman—now running the bookshop for her ailing father—scheduled readings six months in advance these days. She said she'd like me to read parts of my memoir (*this book, Dear Reader*) when we next came to Paris. The bookshop seemed much the same, but *cleaner*—Sylvia dashing around with whiskbroom and dustpan. Sleeping bags and backpacks were still tucked into corners of the upstairs library, and there were the same high bookcases crammed with the poetry and prose, modern and classic, French or English, that George had always encouraged his lodgers to read.

George had sired his daughter at 69. Married to a younger British woman, he claimed his virility was due to eating many slices of butter throughout his meals. Whatever the cause, they had a fine baby girl they'd named for the original Sylvia Beach.

Leaving the store, we walked along Boulevard Montparnasse to Hôtel des Academies, my bargain haunt in the 90s, now sold and remodeled into a several-star hotel—where we were greeted by the smiling manager Cyd, who'd become a good friend. Some 15 years earlier I'd stayed at that little hotel when his first baby was born, and Cyd had attended my first Shakespeare reading the following year.

One warm evening I took Bob over to a party at Jim Haynes' studio, just up the street from Michelle's little apartment. There, for 36 years, Jim, a tall, lanky Louisianan, has served Sunday dinners to half the tourists of Paris. Why? "I like people," he said, "and want them to know each other." He'd found a way to guarantee there would always be new faces for friends and for himself. Whenever in Paris, I tried to go to Jim's—to meet people and have conversations in both English and French.

That Sunday we saw some 50 people spilling out from the studio into the garden where they sat on rocks, benches or folding chairs, balancing dinner plates or wine glasses amidst rose bushes and cherry trees.

After contacting Jim Haynes on his website (www.jim-haynes. com) for a reservation, they'd paid about 30 Euros each—suggested, not required, he said—for wine or juice, a starter soup, green salad and a main dish (chicken pot pie when we were there) with French bread and dessert. All served buffet style in his kitchen. No coffee: "That's too complicated. There might be 50 people," Jim told me. He said he hired or "traded"—sometimes for lodging—a cook. That particular evening, he leaned back in a chair by the stove, welcomed everybody, and introduced them in a hearty voice, discreetly collecting envelopes and checking people's names off a typed list.

He remembered names from the beginning, "Bev West and Bob Royce, this is Pierre Barré; Pierre, Angela Sollini; Angela... etc." When Bob and I walked by a second time, he introduced us again to whoever happened to be standing in the dinner line. Jim's garden was down three steps from the front porch with a brick path leading to about 15 other ateliers. "I always invite the neighbors," he said, "and one or two sometimes come. And I promise them to end the party by 11."

It had been forever since Liz and I hosted our Paris parties. Or had it been just yesterday?

Another evening I introduced Bob to a famous old student restaurant—the Polidor, on rue Monsieur le Prince near the Sorbonne. A hundred and fifty years old. No credit cards. I'd eaten there as a student back in the 50s and a couple of times in the 90s. Good food, simple, with few choices—often a good sign.

We didn't just eat and party in Paris. We went to some museums, too. My favorite has always been the obsolete railroad station, d'Orsay, with its Beaux Arts architecture and magnificent glass ceiling. The French had refused to tear the station down, instead converting it to an impressionist art gallery now housing major works by Manet, Cezanne, Monet, Renoir, Degas, Toulouse-Lautrec, Van Gogh and Sisley. Attention, New York: You could have saved Penn Station with its neo-Roman architecture—now just a basement under Madison Square Garden.

After the Musée d'Orsay, I showed Bob the Pompidou Center with its Brutalist and high-tech architecture, crazy outdoor "plumbing" and 25-foot Calder mobile in front. Then a trip to the

Sorbonne area, where I remembered taking a few classes in the 50s, but spending more time in the nearby cafés. Near the Sorbonne was the Cluny museum with its Gothic but subtly-sexy unicorn tapestries.

Also took a scenic boat tour—the Bateau Mouche—on the Seine, which I'd never done. (Wouldn't have done anything so touristy in my cool 20s.) Michelle's studio was only available for a week, so we spent a few days at a little walk-up hotel, called Myosotis (forget-me-not) on rue Aude, a nearby side street. It was clean, and simple with a great restaurant—again a menu with few choices, all excellent.

A French friend, Christiane, who'd visited Bainbridge, invited us to spend a week with her in her village of Bar sur Loup in the hills above Nice. We rode there on the TGV, an ultra high-speed rail and were met in Nice by Christiane (Kiki), who was dark-eyed and slender. She drove us to her spacious stone house—a gorgeous south of France locale and home—fed us fine meals and showed us many places, including Juan les Pins on the Riviera, where I remembered swimming with Liz and my parents in the 50s. Sixty years later, on this same beach, I lounged with Bob and Kiki on foam cots under beach umbrellas, drank iced tea, and went in and out of the water a dozen times. We were on the *Côte d'Azur* with blue water and the whitest sand I've ever seen.

Kiki maneuvered us and her little Fiat up 1,000 winding feet to the medieval town of Gourdon, and another day down to Antibes on the coast, near Nice. There we saw Les Belles Rives hotel where F. Scott and Zelda had stayed. Another day, she drove us to Saint-Paul-de-Vence and the Maeght Foundation's important collection of modern art. I saw some of my favorites—Georges Braque, Fernand Léger, and Joan Miró—inside the museum and walked through the sculpture-filled gardens. Another day, we peered in at the Monte Carlo gaming tables, but kept our Euros safe in travel pouches, and I didn't dare get caught reading.

We had to leave, of course, and flew to Amsterdam and then Seattle. But saying goodbye to France is, for me, an impossible thing to do. Part of me belongs there and I always have a sick, empty feeling when it's time to leave. I've felt that way at 26, at 76, and now still at 86. Realistically, I like my life in the US with Bob, and wouldn't really want to live alone—even in Europe. But France, Paris in particular, is always nagging at me: the sounds of the language, the smells of just-baked croissants and acrid coffee, the newly-lit Gauloises or Gitanes, the illuminated bridges on the Seine, and of course the cafés, often three on a street and on nearly every corner. You might think writing this book would have cured me, but instead it's just whetted my appetite all the more—to return again to Paris.

Looking back on our houseboat on an Amsterdam canal.

Ghosts Haunt Italian Castle

BY BEVERLY LEHMAN

I lived in a castle—a real one, complete with tower and ramparts (and, I think, even ghosts)—when I visited the Gulf of La Spezia in Italy.

My home was the Castello San Giorgio, an imposing stone structure set high on a cliff overlooking the fishing port of Lerici. It was built in the 16th century for the Italian militia and was used later as a prison for Francois Premier and is now the vacation residence of vagabond travelers from all over the world.

Officially it's a student hostel, but as the term "student" in Europe is loosely defined, ages and occupations vary. When a friend and I were there in October "students" include preschool children, and a monk.

200 Steps to Cl...

It took us several get used to castle every time we wan... up or down, there ... steps to climb, dim... ed passageways ... and a neglected, ... eerie chapel to by...

Sometimes the ... seemed too much ... ly after a luxuri ... vating day on the ... such evenings we ... our own spaghe ... hostel kitchen an... mi-style on the ...

the town of Lerici, the ... tel houses of the town... ple and Lerici's main ... the Albergo della P... There occupants pay ... day. American plan, ... elevator service throv... Castle rates: 35 cents.

The castello has ... bathrooms equipped ... stall showers — cold... but in sunny Italy we ... mind. We slept in ... tories on mattresses ... rubber, comfortable ... by our American sta... Blanket and linen ... provided, although ... hostelers brought ... bags.

Ghosts Intervie...

The matron-hou... is a tiny, wiry ... named Madeleine ... or "Madi." She ... through the roo... day, making beds, ...

Dear M,D,

Just ... middle of ... Features, ... papers an... what they ... It's ... (Peter Du... idea for ... them. It ... and the p... I've ... last few ...

THIS SPACE MAY BE USED FOR WRITING

Dear two (save for this?),

It must be a bit lonely with Daddy away, or are you rather enjoying... during the day and living on... salads and anchovy and...? Mother's... waiting for me...

Liz came in the afternoon, so I feel caught up on the news. Paris is her most beautiful right now, and I wish we could share walks through the Luxembourg and the shopping for croissants each morning. The wonder part is just beginning, although the bits of green haven't yet begun to appear. I think it will all happen in a few weeks — that magic.

I see I'll be flooded with tourists, but no family among them. Do tell them I have to keep early nights. It will be fun to see them. Will Betty and Hughie cross the channel with Marguerite? They haven't seen Paris yet, and it would be a shame to miss it.

Last night I went to a friend's apartment for dinner (Grace Burpett...

FOLD HERE

June 17, 1952

if a quickie as l'm in the
f a story for UNESCO
tion which goes to news-
s in backward areas to lift

signment. I saw the editor
suggested drafting several
val before going to work on
t encouraging project yet
ty good.
st unbearably homesick the
for anything or anyone but

...my love. Talk of gathering greens makes me long for home. Yes, I miss... appear so fast when you live... I've been going to the discussion whether a ski lodge on the border. I have friends going both places at Christmas. Do hope you don't forget Jimie & John moseley). ...mas I'd curl up & die!

Acknowledgments

My mother, **Helen Bolster Lehman**, who carefully saved all my letters from Paris for the book we knew I would someday write. **Peter West**, my son, who told me for years that a book of my travel adventures would encourage older women and inspire younger women to do the same, and said if I didn't write it *he* would.

Mark West, my son, who researched our family history in Ireland and guided me on an exciting trip through Cork—and for having proofread this manuscript meticulously.

Son **Peter's** wife, talented artist **Jennifer**, mother of my first, also talented, grandchildren, **Finn** and **Ariel**.

Son **Mark's** wife, **Zuzana**, exceptional photographer and environmentalist, mother of my dear little grandchildren, **Zoe** and **Matilda**.

Nancy Rekow, my longtime friend, editor and workshop leader, and our workshop colleagues, especially **Sharon Svendsen** and **Dr. Ellen Merenbach** for valuable criticism.

Tracy Vancura, dear friend, who insisted I put my many Paris stories together in a book, **Cliff Vancura**, my gifted art director/designer, who transformed my computer typescript into beautifully printed and illustrated pages for this book.

Dick West, former husband, and good friend, for those many wonderful years in New York, San Francisco and Bainbridge Island with our two beautiful, spirited sons and for helping me remember dates and events for my book.

My sister, **Elizabeth**, who I wish with all my heart were alive to read about our adventures in Paris, and our memories of raising children together in San Francisco.

The late **George Whitman** of Shakespeare & Co. who encouraged writers to read their poetry on his Monday nights with light from Notre Dame.

The late Beat poet **Ted Joans** and his partner, artist **Laura Corsiglia** for making every night in Paris a poetry night.

Christine Gaffiat and **Stephanie von Tacky** of my Wednesday French circle for their skillful corrections of my French translations and accents.

Anita Evans, warm friend, for her patient technical assistance with my computer questions.

David Adler, great coffeemaker and videographer, who helped so much with publicity.

Betsy Leger, my good friend, for her artistic suggestions.

Bob Royce, my partner, who makes every day a joy and prepares delicious meals of vegetables and fish and encourages me to go with him to the gym.

And all my Paris friends who live in these pages.

Notes on the text

In this memoir, I've changed several names and slightly altered circumstances of some people and places.

Linda Orr's poem from "Her Visits" in *A Certain X* (1980) was used with her permission.

I have reprinted stories of mine from the *San Francisco Chronicle*, the *Dallas Times Herald*, the *Los Angeles Times*, Paris edition of the *New York Herald Tribune*, and the *Durango Herald*.

Also, stories and poems of mine from *Gamut*, a Seattle Central Community College magazine, Bainbridge Island Arts & Humanities Council contests and *Exhibition* magazine.

For All the Wrong Reasons

Poems & Stories

Beverley Lehman West

Also by Beverley Lehman West. Print ISBN:0988339676 and 978-0-9883396-7-5, Ebook ISBN: 0988339684 and 978-0-9883396-8-2

Drawing by Michelle Van Slyke